C000156244

DERBY
PAST

Map of Derbyshire drawn by William Hole in 1622 for Michael Drayton's poem *Poly-Olbion*. The accompanying verse reads:

'Of all the Darbian Nymphs of Darwin lov'd the best
(A delicater Flood from the Fountain never flow'd
Then comming to the Towne, on which she first bestow'd
Her naturall British name, her Darby, so againe
Her to that ancient Seat doth kindly inter-taine
Where Marton-brooke, although an easy shallow rill
There offereth all she hath, his Mistriss banks to fill'

In the margin Drayton added 'Darwin, of the British *Doure Guin*, which is White water, Darby from thence, as the place by water'.

DERBY
PAST

Evelyn Lord

Phillimore

1996

Published by
PHILLIMORE & CO. LTD.
Shopwyke Manor Barn, Chichester, West Sussex

© Evelyn Lord, 1996

ISBN 1 86077 022 3

Printed and bound in Great Britain by
BIDDLES LTD.
Guildford, Surrey

Contents

List of Illustrations

Frontispiece: Map of Derbyshire

Acknowledgements

Special thanks to Linda Owen, Librarian and Lisa Bates, Assistant Librarian of the Derby Local Studies Library, and to Kath Clements, John Dallison, Margaret Eaton, Maureen Hughes, Mandy Henchcliffe, Collette Levers, Steve Royle, and Brenda Welbourne, staff at the library without whose encouragement, interest and practical help this book would not exist.

Thanks also to Anne and Les Edmundson, the staff of the Derby Evening Telegraph picture library, G. Petch, Mrs. M. Sargeant of Royal Crown Derby Porcelain, Rolls-Royce plc., Ed Thompson for the Scottish connection, the University of Derby for making this publication possible and especially to Peter Holdcroft of Media Services, to all my students past and present, and to my youngest son Edward Lord for surviving Derby Past.

Illustrations are reproduced by the kind permission of the following; Derby City Museums and Art Gallery, 2-4, 61, 87-8, 131, 134; *Derby Evening Telegraph*, 127, 135, 140; Derby Local Studies Library, 11, 13, 16, 20-1, 25-6, 30-2, 38, 44-5, 55, 62-3, 65, 67-70, 76-7, 88-91, 95-6, 102, 104-5, 118, 122-3, 133, 139-40, 145-7; Dundee Art Galleries and Museums, 49; L. Edmundson, 10, 64, 79, 106, 142; Edward Lord, 9, 46; G. Petch, 132, 136; Rolls-Royce plc, 124-5, 139; Royal Crown Derby Porcelain Company Ltd., 34-6; Scottish National Portrait Gallery, 18; University of Derby, 23-4, 27, 40-2, 66, 71-4, 78, 80, 86, 94, 107, 110-12, 121.

To Edward, Gabriel and Katie,
with love and thanks

Chapter One

The Beginnings—
Prehistoric Derby to Derventio

◆

Derbyshire is a large county covering 1,035 square miles. It divides into two zones, with uplands and bleak moorlands in the north, and lowlands and fertile plains in the south. Derby, its county town, is in the south. It lies in the valley that the river Derwent has carved out for itself as it flows from the old rocks of the uplands to the new rocks of the lowlands at the point where the river changes from being a busy, fast-running, shallow mountain stream to a deep, slow-moving lowland river that meanders through pastures and water meadows.

Derby is situated at the lowest place where the Derwent could be crossed without a bridge. The old ford at the Causey, now replaced by the Causey Bridge, provided an important crossing point in pre-historic times that linked upland and lowland Britain. On the west side of the Derwent the river is joined by the Markeaton brook which with its tributaries crosses a marshy area in the west of the town which in the medieval period was converted into a mill pond. The combined forces of brooks, rivers and tributaries mean that the town has been subjected to serious flooding in the past. It was flooding in the Triassic period, over 195 million years ago, which laid down the foundations on which the modern city of Derby stands. The Triassic floods deposited layers of keuper clay, the red mud containing gypsum, waterstones and bunter sandstones over a pebble base. This is the origin of the sticky red clay found in most gardens in Derby today.

A profile of what lies below Derby's streets shows that it divides into four geological areas with a keuper clay ridge on either side of the Derwent dipping to the alluvial flood plain by the river. On the west side of the town the Markeaton brook flood plain laid down a deposit of solidified mud bordered

by river borne gravels. As the Derwent flowed south through the glacial deposits of the Ice Age it created broad river terraces of gravel overlaid with boulder clay.

One hundred and fifteen thousand years ago the melting of the ice formed a great lake on Sinfin Moor. In this period elephant and hippopotamus roamed over nearby Boulton Moor. Evidence for the existence of these exotic animals in Derby can be seen in the Derby City Museum. Man too was emerging from the swamps and beginning to make crude stone tools. Old Stone-Age axes have been found on the ridges surrounding Derby in Allestree, Chaddesden, and Chellaston. At some point Old Stone-Age man penetrated the deep forest covering the valley floor where the centre of modern Derby lies today and left stone tools at Litchurch, Normanton and Little Chester. Old Stone-Age man dwelt in temporary shelters or caves and followed a nomadic existence pursuing the great herds of animals, so we have no evidence of any Stone-Age dwellings in Derby. A little further north, however, on the Derbyshire border with Nottinghamshire at Creswell Crags, there is abundant evidence of Stone-Age man as cave dwellers in the company of bears and sabre toothed tigers.

About 10,000 B.C. the climate of Britain changed from damp humid conditions to one of dry cold winters and warm summers. Pollen analysis, which is a technique whereby a core of soil is taken out of the ground and the pollen grains in each layer counted, shows that pine and hazel covered the country. Man became a hunter-gatherer— hunting the deer that roamed in the woods, eating the fish that could be caught in the river and the berries from the heathlands.

In *c.*4000 B.C. the climate changed again to mild wet conditions. As the ice caps melted and added their contribution to rivers already swollen with increased rainfall, the sea level rose. As a result of this the land bridge that linked Britain to the continent was severed, and Britain became an island.

In this period man discovered how to domesticate animals, and how to plant crops, harvest them and keep seeds for the next year. These new skills meant that a settled existence was now possible. This period is known as the Neolithic or New Stone Age. The small flint flakes that the New Stone-Age people used have been found at Chaddesden and Allenton, and a little further away at Belper, Breadsall and Duffield, but not in the area where the centre of Derby lies. This was probably still covered with thick forest.

Nevertheless, the New Stone-Age population of Derbyshire was fairly large and well organised. There is evidence of this organisation at Arbor Low in the Peak district which has been rightly described as the Stonehenge of the north. At Arbor Low a stone circle of 50 stones is set within a complex of high banks and deep ditches.

The New Stone Age came to an end when the radical new technology of metal working was introduced. For a time stone and metal tools existed side by side, with the flint nappers imitating bronze tools and weapons in stone, but eventually the superiority of metal tools made stone obsolete. Much of what we used to know about the Bronze Age in Derbyshire came from burials found either in barrows, the large burial mounds that can be seen in the Peak district, or from urnfield cemeteries where cremations were placed in sealed urns and buried. Recent excavations in front of the southern by-pass have changed this. Sites at Aston on Trent, Swarkestone and Willington all contained evidence for a sophisticated Bronze-Age society in the Derby area. Its population were farming the land, producing good metal tools, and were the owners of elaborate golden jewellery. Two patterned gold bracelets were found under a pot in conjunction with a bronze dagger in a scabbard, and Bronze-Age pottery during excavations on the route of the A564 to the south of Derby at Lockington in Leicestershire.

A Bronze-Age monument of especial interest is the Potlock Cursus which was probably a type of race track. The race course was aligned from north to south, and ran for a mile between two parallel ditches set 75 metres apart. At either end were enclosures, which were perhaps the equivalent of the Paddock and Winners Enclosure!

The Bronze Age was followed by another technological revolution, iron smelting. Iron-Age Britain was divided into tribal areas. Derby lay in the tribal area of the *Coritani* which stretched from the Humber in the north to the Welland in the south with its tribal capital at Leicester. Silver coins from the Coritanian kingdom bearing silver horses on them show that it was in existence by 80 B.C. The best evidence for the *Coritani* in the Derby area comes from Willington where an Iron-Age farmstead has been found set in a ditched enclosure. More plentiful evidence comes from the north of the county where Iron-Age hillforts are found on high ground such as Mam Tor.

There is little evidence for prehistoric man settling where the centre of Derby is situated today. This was to change when Britain became part of the Roman Empire. After conquering southern Britain in A.D. 43 the Roman legions pressed north. The legion that marched northwards into Derbyshire was the legendary ninth Spanish legion who later mysteriously disappeared somewhere in the north of the country. The legion's goal in Derbyshire was the lead deposits in the Peak district. In order to get the lead out to where it was needed the river crossings and road junctions had to be protected from hostile natives. Thus the earliest evidence of permanent settlement in Derby was a Roman fort to guard the Derwent crossing.

There were two Roman forts in Derby. The first was on Strutt's Park on the west bank of the Derwent. This was built in A.D. 50-70 and covered about 80 hectares in area. The fort was abandoned in A.D. 80 when a large new fort was built on the other side of the river at Little Chester. The Romans called this fort *Derventio*, and it appears with this name in the third-century *Ravenna* Cosmography which lists important Roman sites across the Empire.

When William Stukeley the antiquarian visited the site in 1721 the fort was still clearly visible. Little remains today, but Stukeley left a valuable record of

1 *(facing page)*   Plan of *Derventio* as seen by William Stukeley in 1721. Drawn by Simon Degg. From *Iter Curiosem.*

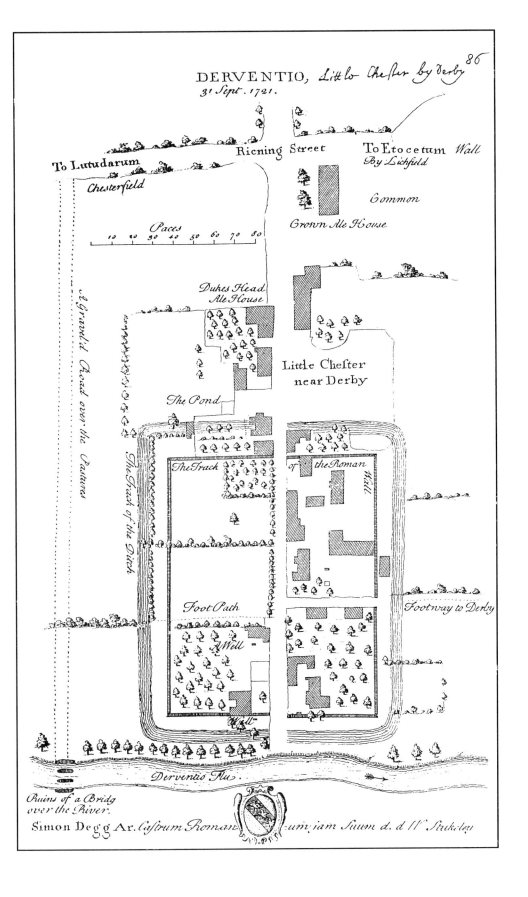

DERVENTIO, *Little Chester by Derby* 86
31 Sept. 1721.

To Lutudarum   Ricning Street   To Etocetum *Wall*
                                              By Lichfield
   Chesterfield

                                        Common
        Paces
   10 20 30 40 50 60 70 80
                              Crown Ale House

                    Dukes Head
                    Ale House

                                   Little Chester
                                     near Derby

         The Pond

                    The Track   of   the Roman

                                                   Wall

         Foot Path   Footway to Derby

                    A Well

                    Derventio Flu.

Ruins of a Bridg
over the River.

Simon Degg Ar. *Castrum Roman... um jam suum d. d. W. Stukeley*

what he saw. On Stukeley's map the north and south gates of the fort can be seen. When the Romans occupied the fort there would also have been gates on the east and west sides of the fort. The line of the footpath shows where these stood.

The fort not only protected the river crossing but it also stood at the junction of five Roman roads. The most important of these was Ryknield Street which linked the west of England with Chesterfield and Doncaster. Excavations have shown that this road was constructed out of gravel set in red mud beneath a layer of gritstone boulders covered with gravel that would have been crushed into the surface by passing traffic. Another important road was the Portway which crossed the river, went through Allestree and then north towards Manchester. The line of this road can be seen at Allestree, and it is probable that it follows the route of an earlier pre-historic trackway that led from the Peak district to southern Derbyshire. Other roads converging on Little Chester went north to Buxton, west to Rocester and south-east to cross the Trent at Sawley. Archaeologists believe that the Romans constructed a bridge across the Derwent in the vicinity of the Strutt's Park Fort, and the 18th-century historian William Hutton claimed that he had felt the piers of this with an oar. However, it is possible that the stones Hutton felt were the remains of Roman wharves that lined the east bank of the river by the fort.[1]

In the fort were barrack blocks built of timber on stone foundations, and a large building which was probably a bath house. This had an under-floor heating system in it, and it is possible that the green-glass perfume bottle discovered at Little Chester is connected to this building. The hypocaust or central heating system now lies under the cricket pavilion on Parker's Piece. Bath houses were normal facilities in all legionary forts, and in this case would have helped the legionaries posted from the warmer parts of the Empire to survive in the chill winds of Derbyshire. The fort also contained shops, shrines and other services that Roman soldiers considered essential such as armourers, taverns and restaurants. In the first century A.D. the fort was contained within a clay rampart which like other Roman fortifications would have been topped by timber battlements and towers. In the second century A.D. the clay rampart was reinforced by a stone wall 8 ft. 9 in. high, and a ditch at least 20 ft. wide.

Two Roman wells have been discovered at Little Chester. One in Marcus Street stood beside Ryknield Street, and the foundations of a building beside it suggest that this may have been a place where travellers could water their horses and take refreshment. The other well is in the garden of the new vicarage of St Paul's church. The Romans also constructed a 90-ft. long stone culvert to drain the fort.

Water was important to the Iron-Age Celts and the Romans. Both had water deities and spirits they worshipped. At *Derventio* evidence for a watery cult comes from a little pewter utensil with a decoration on it in the form of a *nereid*, one of the daughters of Neptune riding through the waves on a sea horse. Other items found in the fort include finely decorated orangey-red pottery known as Samian ware which came from France, and cooking pots made of grey gritty pottery. This pottery is known as Derbyshire ware and it first appears in the second century A.D. By the third century it was

2   Pottery head of a Roman lady with an elaborate hair style. Found at Little Chester, now in the Derby City Museum and Art Gallery.

being exported to military garrisons overseas, and examples of it have turned up in northern France and Spain. Bone combs, iron nails and pins, and grindstones have also been found. One complex that has been excavated has been called the bakers shop because of the quantity of grindstones for milling flour in its vicinity. The shop itself had a paved floor, and a window opening onto the street through which the baker could sell both flour and bread.

Directly outside the fort was a small civilian town where the families of the legionaries and the native Celts lived. This was the normal pattern of development around Roman forts in Derbyshire, and a similar example has been found at Melandra Castle near Glossop in northern Derbyshire. A little further away from the fort at *Derventio* on the old Derby racecourse was an industrial area where smiths, pewterers and potters worked. Again it was normal practice for Roman military and town architects to create an industrial area away from the residential area so that the smoke and pollution could be controlled.

Apart from the fort at *Derventio* and the settlement around it there was a scattering of Roman farmsteads on the lighter soils of the area. A Roman farmstead has been found at Willington lying within a complex of ditched enclosures, and it is possible that there was a Roman farm at Mackworth on the site of Mackworth College. A Roman villa complex has been located at Ockbrook to the east of the town.

The Romans remained at *Derventio* until at least A.D. 350, but the Roman empire was falling apart by that time. In A.D. 409 Emperor Constantine III withdrew the legions from Britain, and in A.D. 410 Emperor Honorius responded to a request for help in defending Britain with an edict which said that Rome could no longer protect its most northerly province. As the Anglo-Saxon Chronicle gleefully recorded, 'never afterwards did the Romans rule in Britain'.[2]

Chapter Two

Saxons, Danes and Domesday

◆

The Romans withdrew leaving a Christian country to the mercy of the pagan Saxons. But it was not an entirely bloodthirsty invasion. The Anglo-Saxon Chronicle reveals that in A.D. 449 the Angles were invited by the Romano-British population of the country to help defend it against invasions from the north by the Picts. It has also been suggested by some historians that Saxons might already have been acting as mercenary soldiers before the Romans left. Liking what they saw, they stayed on, settling near to Roman villas or towns, and were followed by other groups from northern Europe.

The Anglo-Saxon Chronicle describes it thus:

> They then fought against the Picts and had victory wherever they came. Then they sent at once to Angel; ordered them to send more aid and to be told of the worthlessness of the Britons and of the excellence of the land. They then at once sent hither a larger force to help the others.[1]

The main thrust of the Anglo-Saxon movement into Derbyshire came in the fifth and sixth centuries as groups of settlers from North Germany, and Friesland in the Netherlands pushed up the Trent valley and gradually colonised what is now south Derbyshire. At first only small war bands were present imposing a Saxon overlordship on the area. Soon they were joined by their families and retainers. One place that they took over was the Roman farmstead at Willington, where they constructed a hut with a sunken floor to live in. By the seventh century these groups were organised into kingdoms. Derby known to the Anglo-Saxons as Northworthy was the capital of the North Mercians whose territory included Staffordshire north of the Trent, Derbyshire excepting the Peak district and the whole of Nottinghamshire. The

capital of the South Mercians was Tamworth, but eventually north and south Mercia united with a capital at Repton.

Little is known about Northworthy. It is not even clear where it lies in relation to the modern town. One suggestion is that it lay in the area of St Werburgh's Church on a promontory formed by the Markeaton brook, covering the area known today as Jury Street, Bold Lane, the Strand and Victoria Street. Another suggestion is that it stood overlooking the river around the site of the old St Alkmund's Church (by the inner ring road).

Mercia was the last Saxon kingdom to be christianised. This took place in A.D. 653 when Peada, the son of King Penda of Mercia, accepted the Christian faith when he married Elfleda the daughter of the christian king Oswy of Northumbria. Bede recounts that this was the start of missionary work in Mercia. Much of this work came from the churches established in Northworthy. St Alkmund's was the earliest of these, and it probably acted as a centre which sent out priests to other areas in the Midlands.

There were two Saxon saints named Alkmund. One was the Bishop of Hexham who died in 781. The other St Alkmund is more closely connected with Derby. Tradition says that he was the son of King Alured of Northumbria who was killed fighting against King Eadwulf in c.800, and buried at Lilleshall in Shropshire. Very soon miracles were happening at his tomb, and it was decided that as he was a Northumbrian prince he should be removed to his native soil. On the way north either the corpse miraculously expressed a wish to rest in Derby, or the cortège received news of the Vikings' depredations in Northumbria and decided that

3 *(left)* Stone sarcophagus which may have contained the saint's bones. Found in old St Alkmund's Church, now in the Derby City Museum and Art Gallery.

4 *(right)* Saxon cross from old St Alkmund's Church, now in the Derby City Museum and Art Gallery.

Alkmund's remains would be safer in Derby. Here he was buried in the hallowed ground which became St Alkmund's Church, where miracles continued to be performed at his tomb. In the 17th century Michael Drayton recorded another tradition that St Alkmund had been martyred in Derby whilst seeking to convert the heathen Danes. Whoever he was, St Alkmund was revered in Mercia, and several churches were dedicated to him in the Midlands. His feast day is 19 March.[2]

Evidence from excavations done after the demolition of St Alkmund's Church in 1967 shows that the Saxon church on the site could not have been built later than the ninth century. It consisted of a nave and square chancel with two square additions on the north and south sides of the church. Carved Saxon crosses bearing figures of the Evangelists and entwined animals have also been found, as well as the stone sarcophagus which may have contained the body of the saint at one time.

All Saints' Church was founded soon after St Alkmund's, and the dedication to the Saxon saint Werburgh suggests that this church was also founded in the Saxon period. St Werburgh was also a member of a Saxon royal house, a 'most wonderful religious maid' who rid the Soke of Peterborough of a plague of wild geese. Her shrine is at Chester. When Domesday Book was compiled in 1086 there were four churches in Derby.[3]

The Anglo-Saxons left few traces behind them in Northworthy, but we know that their stay came to an untimely end as pagan Vikings surged across the East Midlands.

The Vikings first appeared at Lindisfarne in Northumberland in A.D. 793. For sixty years they harried the country, making lightning raids and then withdrawing with their booty back across the North Sea to their homelands in Scandinavia. The Anglo-Saxon Chronicle records that in 855 'the heathen for the first time wintered in Sheppey'.[4] Twenty years later they had reached Repton, over-run the town of Northworthy and taken it for themselves.

We are not sure where the Viking settlement at Derby was situated. The Roman fort was still standing, and it has been suggested that this is where the Vikings settled. Although we do not know its exact position we do know that the Vikings called their settlement *Deoraby* or Derby, and this name has stuck to the town through the ages.

By is the Scandinavian word for town or village. Derby is the village with a deer park. The deer in its park still features on the city's coat of arms, supported by two further stags which are taken from the Cavendish coat of arms.

It looked as if the Vikings would overrun the whole of the country, but they were eventually defeated by King Alfred of Wessex and the country was divided between the Danes and the Saxons.

5 One of the many representations of the deer within a park fence to be found in Derby. This is a 19th-century version on the Central Library.

Derby lay in the Danelaw, which was an area where the Danish law code prevailed. Derby became one of the Danish five boroughs. The other four were Leicester, Lincoln, Nottingham and Stamford. Only Derby has retained its Danish name.

The name Derby first appeared in documentary evidence in A.D. 917. In that year the Lady Ethelflaede of the Mercians briefly re-took Derby for the Saxons. In the assault four of her favourite thegns were killed within the gates of the town. This information from the Anglo-Saxon Chronicle tells us that Viking Derby was enclosed in some way, and thus it could have been the Roman fort at Little Chester.

The Lady Ethelflaede was a remarkable woman. The 12th-century chronicler William of Malmesbury described her as 'the love of the subject, fear of the enemy, a woman of mighty heart'.[5] She was the eldest daughter of King Alfred of Wessex; a warrior princess who fought beside her thegns in battle. She married Ethelred the Elderman of the Mercians during the 890s. They ruled Mercia as joint monarchs, but as Ethelred was ailing it was the Lady Ethelflaede who took the main part in the crusade against the Vikings. In 907 she fortified Chester against them, and with her brother Edward defeated the norsemen at the Battles of Tettenhall and Wodenfield in 910, and mercilessly pursued them

into Wales. She built a stronghold at Bromesbury, and won the Irish vikings to her side. After Ethelred's death in 911 she ruled Mercia alone. In order to defend her territory she set up a system of defence along the western marches between England and Wales, and along Watling Street and the Fosse Way. In 916 she defeated the Welsh at Brecknock, and it is thought that the King of Gwent fled for refuge behind the walls of Derby, and that is why the Lady attacked it. If she could have held Derby she would have secured the eastern boundary of her kingdom. The Lady Ethelflaede died in 921. She left one daughter, having refused to have any more children, stating that this was unbecoming in a king's daughter. She is reputed to have been buried in St Peter's Church, Gloucester. The Danes were finally driven out of Derby in 942 by Edmund, Lord of the English.

In the late Saxon period Derby was a town of some importance with its own mint. The earliest coins minted in Derby date from the reign of Athelstan in A.D. 925. These coins bear the legend *Deorabi*. Coins continued to be minted at Derby for a further three hundred years. Three coins minted in the reign of William I turned up in the Beaworth hoard of 7,000 coins found in Hampshire. The last coins to be minted in the town were made in the reign of King Stephen, in the mid-12th century. These later coins had four martlets on them and the word *Whichelinus* which was the name of the moneyer who made them. They can be identified as coming from Derby by the inscription 'Derbi' round the edge of the coin.

The town was governed by burgesses who held freehold land in the town and rights of grazing at Quarndon and Little Eaton. There were 13 priests caring for souls in the town, and 14 mills to grind corn and full cloth for the material needs of the townsfolk.

In 1049 this tranquillity was broken by an earthquake, which the Anglo-Saxon Chronicle describes as causing great mortality of men and cattle, and making wild fire spread across Derbyshire doing much damage. This was seen as a portent of horrors to come. The Chronicle records other similar portents leading to the appearance of a mysterious star with a shining tail which hung in the heavens. We now know this to be a manifestation of Halley's Comet, but the Saxons saw it as foretelling the end of the world. It did indeed presage the end of their world with the fall of the last Saxon king, Harold and the Norman Conquest in 1066.

When King Harold was slain at the Battle of Hastings most of the country's landowners and royal officials died with him. They were replaced by William the Conqueror's retainers from Normandy who were rewarded for their part in William's success with lands and offices. One who fought with William was Henry de Ferrers from St Hilaire in Normandy. William gave him vast estates in Derbyshire which he governed from Tutbury Castle. In Derby itself Henry de Ferrers had three residences, and the Ferrers family and Derby were to be closely connected for the next 200 years.

In 1085 the king decided that he would like to know who held the land in his kingdom, and more importantly how much tax he could expect to receive from them. At his Christmas court at Gloucester he declared that he would send men into all counties in the country to find out how much land there was, who had owned it in the time of Edward the Confessor, who owned it in William's days and what it was worth. Pairs of commissioners set out to the four corners of the kingdom. Such were the searching questions they asked, and their severity that they reminded the Saxons of the descriptions they had heard of the Last Judgement. They called the book the commissioners produced Domesday Book.

Domesday Book gives us a picture of life in the towns and villages of Norman England. From the entry for Derby we learn that the number of burgesses in the town had fallen from 243 before 1066 to 140 in 1086, whilst 103 houses in the town stood vacant in 1086. If each burgess was the head of a household of between 4 or 5 people we can estimate that before the Norman Conquest Derby had a population of about 1,100 people. In 1086 this had fallen to a population of about six hundred and thirty. Either many men from Derby had fallen at Hastings, or a dreadful catastrophe such as plague had decimated the town. Trade in the town had been hit as well, as the 14 mills in the town before the Conquest had fallen to 10 by 1086. The town with Litchurch paid £30 in taxes a year. In addition to this the burgesses had to pay the king 144 sheaves of corn for the right to govern the town, restrict who traded there, and to claim exemption from other towns' taxes. A further 43 sheaves were sent to the Abbot of Burton upon Trent who had a mill, arable land and meadow in the town.[6]

The Norman town was built mainly of wood with thatched roofs, but the more important

---

In Derbẏ hī abb̄ de Bertone . I . moliñ . 7 I . maꝰ trǽ
cū ſaca 7 ſoca . 7 II . maꝰ de q̄bꝫ hī rex ſocā . 7 XIII . acꝭ
Goisfriđ alſelin hī . I . ᴁcclam . q̄ fuit Tochi.   Ḻpti.
Radulf̄ . f̄ . Hub̄ti . I . ᴁcclam q̄ fuit Leuric . cū . I . car̄ trᴁ.
Norman de Lincolia . I . ᴁcclam q̄ fuit . Brun
Edric hī ibi . I . ᴁcclam . q̄ fuit Coln patris ej̄
Hugo co̅m̄ hī . II . maſuras 7 I . piſcar̄ cū ſaca 7 ſoca.
Henric̄ de ferrarij̄s . III . maſur̄ cū ſaca 7 ſoca ſimit.
Oſmer pbr̄ hī . I . bou trᴁ cū ſaca 7 ſoca.
Goduin̄ pbr̄ . I . bou trᴁ ſimilit̄

Ad feſtū S Martini reddu̅t burgenſes regi
XII . trabes annonᴁ . de q̄ hī ab̄b̄ de bertone . XL.
Adhuc in eod burgo ſunt . VIII . maſurᴁ ∕ garbas.
cū ſaca 7 ſoca . Hᴁ fuer̄ Ælgar . i̅n ſunt regis.

Duo nū̅mi regis 7 ᵗcius comitis qui exeu̅t de
In Derbeſie   t cenſu
apletreu Wapent . ſunt in manu uicecomitis.
teſtim̄ duarū ſcirarū.
De Stori Anteceſſore Walterij de Aincurt dn̅t
q̄d fine alicuj̄ licentia p̄otuit facere̅ſibi ᴁcclam in
ſua t̄ra 7 in ſua ſoca . 7 ſuā decinā mittere q̄ uel̅let.

4 In DERBY the Abbot of Burton has 1 mill and 1 piece of land with full jurisdiction, and two pieces over which the King has jurisdiction, and 13 acres of meadow.

5 Geoffrey Alselin has one church, which was Toki's.

6 Ralph son of Hubert, one church, which was Leofric's, with one c. of land.

7 Norman of Lincoln, one church which was Brown's.

8 Edric has one church, which was his father Coln's.

9 Earl Hugh has 2 residences and 1 fishery, with full jurisdiction.

10 Henry of Ferrers, 3 residences, likewise with full jurisdiction.

11 Osmer the priest has 1 b. of land with full jurisdiction.

12 Godwin the priest has 1 b. of land likewise.

13 At Martinmas the burgesses pay the King 12 thraves of corn, of which the Abbot of Burton has 40 sheaves.

14 Further, there are 8 residences in this Borough with full jurisdiction. They were (Earl) Algar's; now they are the King's.

15 The King's two pennies and the Earl's third which come from Appletree Wapentake in Derby(shire) are in the Sheriff's hand, or dues; witness of the two shires.

16 Of Stori, Walter of Aincourt's predecessor, they state that he could make himself a church on his land and in his jurisdiction, without anyone's permission and dispose of his tithe where he would.

6   Extract for Derby from Domesday Book.

buildings would have been built of stone, and substantial citizens would have lived in stone houses. Often the living quarters in these were on the first floor, reached by an outside staircase. Livestock or goods were kept on the ground floor, and the front of this floor could be opened up to form a shop. Upstairs the family lived in one large room with a hearth in the centre of the floor, and a hole in the roof to allow smoke to escape.

The population of the town would have been increased by country folk bringing their produce to sell in the Great Market which stood in the area bounded by Full Street, Irongate, and Sadlergate, where the modern market place lies. Men at arms would have thronged the town's streets, as in common with most Norman towns Derby was a garrison town with a castle and strong defences protecting it.

No trace of the castle can be seen today, but William Hutton recorded that in 1791 vestiges of it, consisting of a mound some 80 yards long which ran parallel to Cockpit Hill, could be seen in an orchard. This was guarded on one side by the Derwent, and on the other it overlooked the road from London. A century later in 1895 remains of the castle walls were still visible in Siddalls Road. The street names Castle Street and Copecastle Square in the Eagle Centre show us where the castle and its environs once stood. The area to the south of the Eagle Centre was known as Castle Fields.[7]

The parish church for the castle was St Peter's which was connected to the rest of the town by a ribbon development of houses. The main residences and shops of the town clustered around All Saints', St Alkmund's and St Werburgh's churches. The whole would have been enclosed within defensive walls, either made of stone, or of an earthen bank with a wooden palisade on the top. Such defences were important in the anarchy of the civil war that followed the death of the last Norman king Henry I, when King Stephen and the Empress Matilda fought over the crown. Robert Ferrers, the son of Henry de Ferrers and the principal magnate in Derby, supported King Stephen. In 1138 he was rewarded for this support with the Earldom of Derby.

Robert's grandson, another Robert Ferrers, was to lose the earldom. His parents William and Margaret, the co-heir of the earldom of Winchester, died when he was still young and Robert became a

7 19th-century drawing of Robert de Ferrers' seal. The original is on BL Ms. Cott. Nero D. 1.

royal ward. When Robert was nine the king, Henry III, arranged a marriage between him and the daughter of his half-brother Hugh of Lusignon. They were married in Westminster Abbey in 1249. Robert's bride was aged seven at the time.

During Robert's minority his Derby estates were governed by the King's eldest son, the Lord Edward who later became Edward I, and Henry's queen. Robert came of age in 1260 and entered into full possession of his estates. Such was his treatment at the hands of the royal family that he became a firm supporter of Simon de Montfort in his fight against the king and his struggle for a more democratic way of government. The king regarded Robert with especial disfavour for this.

In 1263 Robert captured three castles from the Lord Edward, but in retaliation the Lord Edward devastated the Ferrers estates in Derbyshire. Between 1265-6 Robert was imprisoned in the Tower of London, and deprived of his estates. On his release he fled to Derbyshire to raise an army against the king. He was defeated by the King's brother and taken prisoner. Generously the king offered to restore the Ferrers estates if Robert paid a fine of seven years' rent. When he did not come up with the money the Earldom of Derby and the Ferrers estates were granted to the king's second son Edmund, Earl of Lancaster. Robert died dispossessed and in poverty on 20 November 1279. His son John

became Lord Ferrers of Chartley, and his daughter married David ap Griffith, a member of the royal house of Wales.

The Ferrers property in Derby became part of the estates of the earldom, later dukedom of Lancaster, and were to become crown property when Henry IV who was the heir to the Duchy of Lancaster became king in 1399. Thus, the town became a royal manor. The borough officials were then required to send the rents of the crown properties in Derby to London, and the borough records include a number of receipts from crown officers for money received from them. Collecting and delivering the rents was an onerous task for the burgesses, but, as we shall see, their advantages over other citizens in medieval Derby more than made up for this.

Chapter Three

Commerce and Churches—Medieval Derby

◆

Medieval Derby was a centre bustling with trade, attracting people from the surrounding countryside and other towns. In 1334 the town had to pay £30 in taxes which was far more than any other town in Derbyshire. The 1377 poll tax shows that there were some 1,076 adults, excluding churchmen, in the town, which suggests a total population of at least 3,000 souls. Another imposition the town was obliged to pay came in 1341 for the provision of 200 white bows and 500 arrows as part of the English war effort in the Hundred Years War.

The burgesses of Derby were rich and powerful, governing the town through two bailiffs chosen annually from their number. They met to transact business in the Moot Hall, which was situated in the Market Place. Moot comes from the Anglo-Saxon word for council. The council room was on the upper storey of the building with shops underneath it.

In 1446 the burgesses were given the right to appoint a borough recorder or judge who with two bailiffs could preside over a Court of Record and try petty cases. This improved the town's status, and perhaps more importantly provided an additional income for the town which could put the fines levied in the court into its treasury.

The burgesses had rights and monopolies in the town which they had obtained through a royal charter. The first evidence of a written version of this comes from the reign of Henry III when in 1229 the king at his court in Westminster granted rights and liberties to his burgesses of Derby. However, it is possible that an earlier charter had already been granted to the town by Henry's father, King John, as the charter confirms liberties already held by the burgesses.

The 1229 charter gave the burgesses the right to hold a weekly market which was to run from Thursday to Friday evening. The main function of this market was probably to sell cloth as the charter also forbade the sale of cloth at these times at any other place within 10 leagues (30 miles) of Derby, except Nottingham. The burgesses were also given the right to hold fairs at Easter, Whitsun and Michaelmas.[1]

By 1330, as well as the Thursday to Friday market, there were also weekly produce markets held on Monday and Wednesday. As well as the Great Market in the centre of the town a subsidiary market grew up in the vicinity of Friargate.

Medieval markets clustered around the market cross. As a symbol of this a headless cross has been moved close to the cross-roads of the Ashbourne and Old Uttoxeter roads. It is known as the Plague

8 In the 19th century the Headless Cross was moved to the Arboretum as shown in this drawing of 1891.

9 Swarkestone Causeway which crosses the Trent flood plain was built in the medieval period. It was essential to the trade and communications of Derby as it connected the town to London and the south of the country.

Cross, as tradition says that in times of plague vinegar was placed in the hollow at the top of the cross to disinfect coins which country folk could take in exchange for leaving food for the stricken town. In 1426 the headless cross was recorded as standing in the Parkfield.

As well as the market crosses there are three further crosses mentioned in medieval documents. One is the Whitecross which has given its name to Whitecross Street to the west of Kedleston Road; another is Chaddesden Cross. The third is described as the Palmer's Cross which marked the boundary of Litchurch and Derby. Palmer was a word signifying pilgrim. Making a pilgrimage to a shrine containing holy relics was an important feature of medieval life. Many pilgrims would have visited the shrine of St Alkmund in Derby, but the ultimate goal of the pilgrim was of course Jerusalem. One medieval citizen of Derby may have made that journey as he was known as Gilbert the Palmer who lived in the Newlands between 1233 and 1248.

In the Great Market were fixed stalls, some owned by the burgesses and passed down from parents to children. Nigel son of Baldwin left his three daughters Emma, Helwise and Leticia a stall apiece. Emma and Helwise's stalls were 16 ft. long and 11 ft. wide, but Leticia's was 36 ft. long and 8 ft. wide. Many of the stall holders were women. In 1200, Avice Raven had a stall next to those of Robert Colle and Ralph son of Walkelin. By 1214 Robert Colle had extended his business and had two shops on the east side of the market where he

had as neighbours shops owned by Henry son of Herbert, Thomas Juvenis and Walkelin son of Cecilie. Another successful entrepreneur was Henry de Lorimer who in 1248 had a stall and two shops in the market place between the stall and shops of Hugh son of Herbert and Robert de Sallow.

We do not know what the market stalls sold, although Henry de Lorimer could have sold bits for horses' bridles as his surname means bit-maker. But we do know from the street names the trades and commodities sold in Irongate and Sadlergate. In 1250 three occupants of Sadler Street, as it was called then, were Roger de Lyndesby, Nicholas Lorimer who was probably connected with the saddlery and harness trade, and Lawrence the Saddler.[2]

Other tradesmen in medieval Derby reflect the importance of cloth working in the town. Dyers colouring cloth were to be found, as were fullers bleaching the cloth in fulling mills along the Derwent. All manner of crafts and trades were present in the town. These ranged from coopers making barrels for ale, glove-makers and goldsmiths providing luxury items for the wealthy citizens and gentry.

Although the town was thronged with people, and houses and shops huddled together within its walls, life was still close to the land and agriculture. The town was surrounded by fields which were cultivated by the townsfolk. Each burgess had a number of strips of land in vast open fields in which corn, oats and pulses were grown in rotation. Beside the Derwent lay lush water meadows where cattle could graze and hay was produced, and at Litchurch was common pasture available for all the town's livestock.

Darley Abbey also farmed land in the town. It had a great barn situated on what today is Abbey Street. It also owned a considerable amount of property in the town including houses with land attached to them, three mills and a fishery on the river. Much of Darley Abbey's property in the town was leased out to tenants. The details of these leases and of the property transactions made between the Abbey and its tenants are recorded in the *Darley Abbey Cartulary* which is a collection of deeds that belonged to the abbey. From this collection of documents we know something about the ordinary people living in medieval Derby.

Between the 1170s and 1210 Edwin Starolf and Robert son of Gode leased part of the fullers' land where raw cloth was stretched out to be bleached. Adwisa Saleman worked the Twigrist mill, and John de Mildenton had land beside the mill. William Basset, John Ironmonger, William Barr, Hammond the Clerk and Sister Alice of Derby had land which lay between the Derwent and St Michael's cemetery. In Full Street lived Geoffrey the king's official, Emma Riden, John Gryn, Robert Ouleape, Richard the Carpenter and William of Nottingham. William of Nottingham also had land in Altunsditchfield and Cappecroft with Robert le Worm, William of Rowditch and Thomas Juvenis who owned a shop in the market place as his neighbours. Henry de Lorimer who had shops and stalls in the market also had farm land in the fields of Middlefurlong, Doggelowe and Newlands.[3]

The land was usually parcelled out in selions. Each selion was a cultivated ridge of arable land in the town's open lands. For example in 1291 Roger de Tickhill had five selions in the Ditchfield, Matilda de Trowell four, and William Spon three. William Spon's selions abutted the Darley Abbey Grange, so it is probable that the Ditchfield was in the Abbey Street area, and the ditch referred to is the ditch marking the town boundary and defence. Close to Abbey Street is Newlands Street, and many of the grants and leases made by the abbey were for house sites and land on the Newlands. In 1240 Emma de Darley lived next door to her sister Hawise on the Newlands, and was separated from a third sister Mariota by Nicholas the Carter. On the other side of Mariota lived Richard de Macleff and Emma de Lafful. Twenty years later in 1261 we learn that Robert son of Robert, Nicholas the Carter, William at the Bridge, John Cayn and William Swift were neighbours on the Newlands by the bend of the Scolebrooke.[4]

The names of the people mentioned in the leases and grants can tell us something about them. Many are described as son or daughter of ...; for example Nicholas son of Henry had land in the Newlands in 1233 and Matilda daughter of Robert the Dean had a house in Walker Street where her neighbours were Simon son of Susannah and William of Coventry. The latter tells us where William came from, and there are many people described in this way. William had probably travelled the furthest but others had come from Stoke, Stamford, and Castleton as well as from places closer to Derby such

as Kirk Langley and Quarndon. Others came from Donington and Ashby in Leicestershire and Trowell in Nottinghamshire.

The deeds can also tell us about the person's trade. There are smiths, ironmongers and wheel-wrights as well as dyers, a skinner and a glovemaker mentioned in the documents. Bakers, coopers, hoopers and a cowman show that the food and drink trades were also represented in medieval Derby. Hugh the Cooper, Henry the Cowman, William Cubboc and William of Chaddesden were all neighbours on the Hey which would have been a meadow area for grazing livestock and providing hay for fodder.

During the 14th century one citizen of Derby buried treasure and did not have chance to reclaim it, leaving it to be discovered six hundred years later in 1927 when workmen digging foundations in City Road found an earthenware jug containing over 500 coins dating from the reigns of Edward I to Edward III, 1272-1377. Most of these coins were silver pennies or half pennies and were minted in a number of places across England, Ireland and Scotland. The hoard also included silver 'sterlings' from Flanders. Why the hoard was buried can only be conjectured. It has been suggested that it was part of the Burton Abbey treasury buried at the time of the Dissolution of the Monasteries, but it is more likely that the money was the proceeds of a robbery hidden by the thief.[5]

Darley Abbey was the most important religious house in the Derby area. It grew out of an oratory or small chapel where mass could be sung which was dedicated to St Helen, that had been given to the town by Towyne a burgess in 1137, and was staffed by Austin canons. In 1154 Robert de Ferrers created the abbey at Darley and some of the St Helen's canons under their Abbot Albinus moved there. The abbey had a garden and courtyard, and by 1308 was surrounded by 240 acres of arable land, and six acres of meadow. The ridge and furrow which shows where the monks' ploughs passed can still be seen in Darley Abbey Park. The abbey also had two mills on the Derwent and a pigeon house. As well as land in Derby and its environs, the abbey had mills and land in Aldwark, Bolsover, Butterley, Glapwell, Ripley, Scarcliffe, Wessington and Youlgreave. In 1251 Henry III visited the abbey and during his stay granted it the right to hold a market and fair in Ripley, and permission to build

10   The Guest House at Darley Abbey is the sole remaining monastic building. Now converted into a public house it still shows the first floor entry and the undercroft characteristic of many medieval buildings. Similar examples would have been common in the centre of Derby during the medieval period.

a rabbit warren. The Abbots of Darley were chosen by the crown with the agreement of the canons at Darley. St Helen's hospital continued as a house of God administered by Darley, but disappeared from the records in 1306 when it was probably absorbed into the abbey.

Kings Mead Priory or the Nunnery of St Mary *Pratis* as it was sometimes known was founded by Darley Abbey in *c*.1160 when its care was assigned to Abbot Albinus by Bishop Walter Durdent. The first prioress was Emma, and she was helped by a chaplain called William de Bussel. In 1230 the nunnery was given 13 acres of arable, and pasture for 300 sheep and lambs, eight oxen, six cows, 30 goats and 20 pigs by Lancelin Fitzlancelin and Avice his wife. Other land was also given to the nunnery, and its growing wealth caused strife between the nunnery and Darley Abbey on which Bishop Roger de Weskham had to arbitrate in 1250. The nunnery's hospitality was so popular with travellers that its

coffers became depleted. In 1327 the nuns were forced to ask the king for help because of this, and also because a cattle murrain had hit their herds. The king appointed Robert Alsop and Simon of Little Chester to help the nuns, but they were still in debt when prioress Joan Touchet died in 1349, probably a victim of the Black Death. The prioresses were usually member of gentry families, a fact that Elizabeth Stanley was not slow to point out when bailiffs tried to distrain against the nunnery for debts. Other gentry families represented at the nunnery were the Beresfords, Mackworths and Knowles.[6]

St Leonard's Hospital for Lepers was founded *c*.1220 by Henry II. It lay outside the town walls in order to cut down the risk of infection. A commission of inquiry into its operation in 1316 revealed that, although those admitted to serve in the hospital were required to swear vows of obedience, poverty, chastity and secrecy, they were not required to wear habits or to attend set prayers.

The hospital was funded mainly from its flock of 300 sheep.[7]

A tax of 1202 records that there were 66 monks in Derby. Some lived in a small Cluniac priory of St James. This consisted of a prior and two monks and had an annual income of £5 4s. 8d. The Cluniacs were a French order and unpopular during the French wars. This may have been the cause of a disturbance which took place in 1289 when three priests from All Saints' broke down the priory doors, beat the prior and stole his property. A rental of 1532 shows that the priory had land in Charnwood Forest as well as tenements and closes in Derby. It also received rent on St James's Day from the Chamberlain of Derby for right of passage over St James's Bridge across the Markeaton Brook. This was one of the 10 bridges over the brook, and it connected St James to the Wardwick.[8]

In 1224 a Dominican friary of 20 'black monks' was opened in what today is Friargate. A number of Italians were amongst the first friars, including Brother *Ruffolo* who died whilst on a visit to Nottingham. As he lay dying he had a vision of St Edmund and the Blessed Virgin and was heard to confess his sins to them. Royal visitors to Derby often stayed at the Friary. These included Edward II who took refreshment there in 1323, and Henry IV who spent two nights with the friars in 1403. Although the friars were an open preaching order who would have been well known in the town, they do not seem to have been popular. In 1344 a large body of at least 48 men broke into the Friary, carried off goods and chattels and wounded the friars' servants. Those who were indicted for this crime included a number of local tradesmen and merchants. A 17th-century map shows that the friary had extensive grounds of at least eight acres, and its own graveyard.[9]

As well as the monastic foundations medieval Derby was well served with churches. The short-lived St Mary's Church was given by William I to Burton Abbey with a mill and cottages to sustain it, but disappeared from the records early in the medieval period. Later the dedication St Mary was given to the Bridge chapel.

All Saints' and St Alkmund's were collegiate churches. This meant that there were priests in these

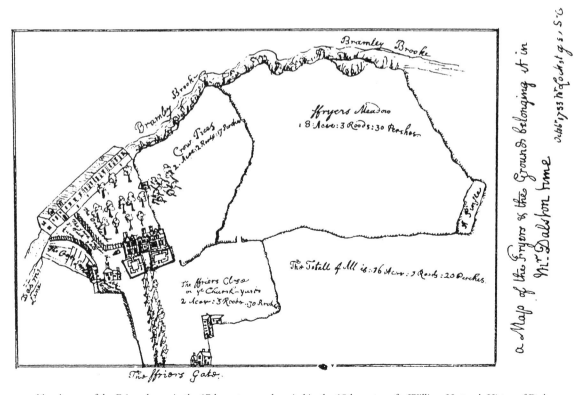

11   A map of the Friary drawn in the 17th century and copied in the 18th century for William Hutton's *History of Derby.*

12 St Mary's Bridge Chapel in the 19th century.

probably the most wealthy parish because of its position close to the market and shops. Evidence of this wealth comes from the magnificent Perpendicular tower built by the parishioners at the beginning of the 16th century. It is arguably the highest and one of the most beautiful examples of this style of tower in the country. Daniel Defoe, writing in the 18th century, records that the tower was built at the request of the bachelors and maidens of the parish, and that whenever a maid was wed in the church only bachelors rung the bells. Whether this is true is not known, but the north and south sides of the tower bear the inscription 'young men and maidens', although words missing from this might indicate that it is in fact an extract from the scriptures rather than a dedication.[10]

churches who sang masses perpetually for the souls of the dead. These 'colleges' of priests have given their name to College Street which is close to All Saints' Church. The collegiate priests of All Saints' were remunerated from the rents and incomes of property in the town, and in the 16th century from five farms in Little Chester.

Between St Alkmund's and All Saints' lay the smaller, poorer parish of St Michael. All Saints' was

Inside All Saints' Church were three chantry chapels where priests sang masses for the souls in torment. These were the Chantry of Our Lady which was founded by the Dean of Lincoln, Will Shore's chantry where a priest sang before the altar of St Nicholas, and the Holy Trinity Guild chapel which was maintained by the bailiffs and burgesses

13 All Saints' Church from the west.

14 'Green Man' medieval carving on All Saints' tower.

of the town in order that a priest could say a mass before the Trinity at five o clock each morning for the lives and souls of all the brothers and sisters in the guild.

St Alkmund's medieval church has gone, demolished to make way for the ring road, and apart from its tower All Saints' was totally remodelled in the 18th century. St Werburgh's and St Michael's churches were also remodelled. Only St Peter's Church and the Bridge chapel retain any medieval fabric. Apart from these there is little visible evidence of medieval Derby left, although the street plan in the centre of the town follows the line of the medieval streets, and the street names show where the medieval citizens lived and worked.

15 19th-century engraving of the medieval inscription 'young men and maidens' from All Saints' which can still be seen high up on the north wall of the tower.

16 St Peter's Church.

Chapter Four

Tudor Derby

The 16th century was a period of change, both in the country as a whole and in Derby. In his effort to gain a divorce from his first wife Katharine of Aragon, Henry VIII broke with the Roman Catholic faith, dissolved the monasteries in 1536 and embraced the Protestant church. Before closing the monasteries a commission of inquiry was sent out to see how much yearly income each religious house could expect. A priest named James Billingsford visited Darley Abbey and Kings Mead Nunnery. He put fear into the hearts of the monks by claiming that he had heard a rumour that they had sent their treasure overseas in a wool pack in order to prevent the king getting it. He also terrified the nuns of Kings Mead by demanding in a most abrasive manner to count the sisters, and to see their livestock in the barns which caused the Abbot of Darley to write to the king to complain.[1]

The commission found that Darley Abbey was the wealthiest monastery in the Derby area, worth £258 14s. 5d. a year. The nunnery was worth only £38 14s. a year. Joan Curzon, the daughter of the local family from Kedleston, was the last prioress of the nunnery. After the nunnery was closed it was purchased by the Earl of Shrewsbury who sold it to a wealthy yeoman family, the Suttons. They paid £181 3s. 6d. for it. The nunnery lands were used for farming and the gatehouse converted into a dwelling. In 1543 Thomas Sutton added to his lands with 20 acres of meadow in Kings Mead, five acres in Nuns' Close, six acres of pasture in St Mary's Close, and three acres of pasture called New Close.[2]

Darley Abbey was dissolved in 1538. The church, Lady chapel with its bell and other monastic buildings and their contents were sold off, and the monks were given pensions out of the proceeds.

The Abbot received £50, and 26s. 3d. was awarded to Thomas Tutman the schoolmaster at the abbey. The site was granted to Robert Sacheverell, and then to Sir William West.

The Friary in Friargate was let to John Sharpe of London at an annual rent of 54s. The main buildings became a private residence but the friars' graveyard remained, and became a lure for light-fingered thieves such as Richard Canderdyne, a labourer who broke into the Friary grounds and stole marble, lead and iron worth £4.

Although John Sharpe was a Londoner he tried to interfere in local politics. In 1546 a supplication was made to the Privy Council by William Allestree and other citizens of Derby claiming that factions within the burgesses had made an illegal attempt to make Sharpe a burgess, and to disenfranchise Thomas Warde and William Bulkeley the sitting bailiffs.[3]

The colleges of priests who sang the perpetual masses for the souls of the dead in All Saints' and St Alkmund's churches were disbanded. However, in 1554 Queen Mary, who restored the Catholic church, reinstated them. She gave the bailiffs and burgesses of the town a large gift of land and property, the rents from which were to maintain perpetual vicars in All Saints' and St Alkmund's.

Not everyone in Derby wished to return to the old faith. In 1556 a blind girl Joan Waste was burnt to death in the Windmill Pit for clinging to the Protestant faith.

Joan was aged only 22 when she died. She was the daughter of William Waste a barber of All Saints' parish. Although blind from birth she learnt how to knit and turn ropes, and out of her earnings from these she saved up and purchased a New Testament in English. She employed an elderly prisoner John Hurt, who was in prison for debt, and John Pemerton the parish clerk of All Saints' to read it to her daily, and soon she had many passages of it by heart which she would recite. She also entered into disputation about the scriptures with others, for which she was accused of heresy, for not believing that the sacrament was the body of Christ, and for saying that Christ's blood could not be converted into bread and wine. She was threatened with torture but would not recant her beliefs. She was tried before a panel of judges that included Ralph Baines the Bishop of Coventry and Lichfield, local gentlemen such as Sir John Port and Henry Vernon, and a Derby official named Peter Finch. They found her guilty of the crime of heresy and condemned her to death by burning at the stake.

She was taken into All Saints' Church and made to stand at the front of the congregation whilst a sermon was read against her. Then she was taken out of the church to her death. Her brother Roger held her hand and led her to the place of execution, down Sadlergate, past St Werburgh's Church and into the Windmill Pit where she was tied to the stake, faggots piled around her and the torch applied. She died crying on Christ to have mercy on her.

Joan Waste was not the only martyr to die for her faith in 16th-century Derby. In 1583 three Catholic priests, Nicholas Garlick, Robert Ludlam and Richard Simpson, were discovered hiding in a fireplace in the chapel of Padley Hall. They were tried at Derby for treason and espousing the Roman Catholic faith which had been outlawed by Elizabeth I, found guilty and hung, drawn and quartered which was the usual punishment for traitors. Their bodies were placed on poles on the approaches to St Mary's Bridge as a warning to others, and today there is a memorial to them on St Mary's Bridge chapel. In December 1588, 37 Roman Catholics who would not give up their faith were imprisoned in a small and smelly place over the Oddbrook in the Cornmarket. Such was their privation that three prisoners died: Richard Kitchen a husbandman or smallholder, Richard Spencer a yeoman, and Humphrey Beresford a barrister. James Clayton a priest who visited them to administer comfort was also imprisoned and died in gaol.

The county of Derbyshire as a whole had many unrepentant Catholics in it. The Peak district in particular was noted by Thomas Becon a puritan divine as being a hotbed of catholicism. It is also known that John Ramridge, the Archdeacon of Derby, did not sign the Act of Uniformity which sanctioned the adoption of the revised *Book of Common Prayer* in 1559, but other clergymen in Derby did subscribe to the act, and St Peter's Church appointed a licensed preacher to give sermons four times a year. Richard Kilby, the curate of All Saints' from 1609-17, was a noted puritan and a man who believed in plain speech. During his incumbency he wrote in the parish registers that he saw no reason why a register for English people should not be written in that tongue. His devotion to his flock was recorded in his epitaph, now unfortunately lost but noted down in the early 19th century:

> Loe, Richard Kilby lieth here
> Which lately was our ministere
> To the poore he ever was a friend,
> And gave them all he had at's end.
> This towne must twenty shillings pay
> To them for him each Good Friday,
> God graunt all Pastors his good mind
> That they may leave good deeds behind
> He dyed the XXIst of October 1617[4]

Presentments of Catholics made to the Quarter Sessions reinforce the picture of a Catholic county but Protestant county town. In 1632 there were 158 Catholics reported in the High Peak hundred, but only 33 for the combined hundreds of Litchurch and Morleyston in which Derby lay.

Queen Mary also revived the Free School. Such a school had existed in the medieval period but had fallen into disuse. Queen Mary decreed that it was to be maintained by the bailiffs and burgesses from her grant. They were to pay the master and usher £13 16s. 8d. a year. The Free School founded by Queen Mary was located in St Peter's churchyard

17   The Free School as seen at the end of the 18th century.

and is now the Heritage Centre. The first recorded master was Richard Johnson.

It was close to the Free School that the other Queen Mary, the tragic Queen of Scots, stayed when she spent a night in Derby in 1585. She was being taken from Sheffield to Tutbury Castle by her keepers. Her governor, Sir Ralph Sadler, felt that she had travelled far enough for one day and that she should rest the night in Derby. He sent instructions ahead to the town that no assembly of people was to be allowed whilst the queen was present, and during the night eight constables patrolled the streets to ensure that a curfew was enforced.

Mary was lodged in the house of a respectable widow, Mrs. Beamont, who with four mature neighbours acted as Mary's maids in waiting for the night. During her stay Mary was not allowed to speak with any other townspeople, and left the next morning to continue to her damp and unhygienic lodgings in Tutbury Castle. Sir Ralph was soundly rebuked by Queen Elizabeth for his humanitarian action in allowing Mary to stay overnight in the town.

Plague was an ever present fear in Tudor and Stuart Derby. The town suffered outbreaks in 1586 and 1592. The latter outbreak began in the house of William Sowter a butcher of All Saints' parish, and quickly spread to St Alkmund's parish. This was a particularly severe outbreak which lasted until 1593. In St Werburgh's parish alone, where the usual annual burial rate was eight people, this rose to 65 for the year 1592–3.

Another outbreak of the plague occurred in 1636. This time it started in Bag Lane and spread to all areas of the town. Plague was to reappear in 1665. During this occurrence the town went into quarantine. Grass grew in the deserted streets, and the country folk would go no further than the headless cross to deliver their produce. There they picked up the coins steeped in vinegar as disinfectant placed in the hollow depression on its top. Many townspeople died and trade in the town was at a standstill.

At the end of the 16th century the plight of the poor in the town was becoming desperate. As well as each parish in the town levying a poor rate and paying poor relief to its paupers, individuals bequeathed money to be put towards helping the

18   Mary, Queen of Scots.

poor. In 1529 Robert Liversage a dyer and burgess of Derby set up a charity in his will which was to help the poor of St Peter's parish. He gave the rents from his property in St Peter's, the Cornmarket, on the Morledge and in Wanndell and Bag Lanes to the Vicar and Churchwardens of St Peter's and a body of trustees to be used for the poor. Almshouses were built, and bread and ale dispensed to the poor of St Peter's parish. Bess of Hardwick endowed almshouses in 1597 for eight poor old men and four women. Bess died in 1607 and was buried in the magnificent tomb she had planned for herself in All Saints'. One of the tasks of the occupants of her almshouses was to keep the tomb clean and tidy.

Tudor and Stuart Derby was not an altogether peaceful place. All too often violence and riot could spill out on to the streets. In 1545 there was a riot in St Peter's Church when an attempt was made to kidnap a youthful Mr. Curzon who was a ward of court. As the disturbance began to get out of hand

19   19th-century drawing of Bess of Hardwick's tomb in
All Saints' Church.

the town hall bell was rung to summon the burgesses
to assist in restoring order. The gentry caused another
disturbance in 1576 when a great number of
retainers were assembled by Sir John Zouche and
Sir Thomas Stanhope to settle a private feud in the
town's streets. Again the town hall bell was rung
and order restored by the burgesses. A further affray
happened in 1588 between Mr. Vernon's and Mr.
Longford's men. Once more the town hall bell
summoned aid and the burgesses parted the
squabbling factions. A year before this a great flood
had inundated the town, broken down the great
bridge and carried two mills clean away.

A little later in 1601 St Werburgh's Church
steeple fell down, perhaps an omen of the upheavals
which were to follow. The same year a body of
soldiers from Lincolnshire en route for Ireland
terrorised the town and prevented people from going
to church. During 1601 two women were burnt to
death in the Windmill Pit for poisoning their

husbands. This was the normal punishment inflicted
on a wife for poisoning her spouse.

Two years later between 1602-3 the burgesses
themselves were in continuous disagreement with
private landowners who enclosed common grazing.
Fences were torn down, and riots against the
enclosures followed. Further disorder was to bring
lasting disgrace on the town when in 1610 a great
argument between Sir Philip Gresley and Sir George
Stanhope spilled out into the town's streets where
the populace took sides against each other. Such
was the controversy and threat of public disorder
that the judges who were present for the Assizes
decided that the town was not a safe place, and the
Assizes were removed to the tranquillity of
Ashbourne.

At the end of the 16th century the town had
a population of at least 2,000 people. Many of these
were craftsmen, tradesmen and retailers living in and
around Sadlergate. Richard More a weaver lived in
Sadlergate with his neighbours Francis Morris, a
maltster, and Stephen Slighe, a glover. Other tradesmen in Tudor Derby included William Atterley,
William Sowter, Thomas Wallace, John Watson and
Thomas Whyterrans who were all butchers.
Supplying other items of food and drink were
William Grene, a baker, John Taylor of the *Market
Inn*, whilst the aptly named Eliazer Hakes sold fish
to the town. Robert Potter and Cecilie Burdon
owned kilns and malthouses in St Peter's parish,
whilst Richard Ward and Robert Winter of St Peter's
Bridge, Thomas Greave of Market Street, Edmund
Bown, John and Matthew Bate were all iron-
mongers. The Elizabethan citizens of Derby could
buy gloves from Edward Walker of Parkfield, and
clothes from Robert Lonte a tailor living on the
Morledge. Other tailors in the town were Ralph
Melbourne, Henry Sacheverell and Anthony Spyser.

The tailors and clothworkers had their own
companies whose guardians looked after their
interests in the town, stopping outsiders from
trading, fixing prices and making sure that debts to
their members were paid on time. Trade in
Elizabethan England depended to a large extent on
trust and credit. The business of Lawrence Brynnley
the Guardian of the Clothworkers was no exception
to this. In 1597 we find him being sued in the
borough Court of Pleas for an unpaid debt of 39s.
owed to Robert Brownell. Robert Brownell was

one of the town bailiffs for that year. As well as suing Lawrence Brynnley for debt he also sued William Stevens a smallholder of Heanor for a debt of £80. Between 1590-9 Robert Brownell was to sue 14 people in order to recover debts. Amongst other debts he was owed £40 by Ralph Blackwell a gentleman from Wensley, £10 10s. by Robert Bainbridge, and £20 by Anthony Bludworth of Heanor. The largest amount owed to him was £200 which he claimed from William Buckley and Thomas Fytch the executors of William Beamont who had died in debt.

Women are less visible than men in Elizabethan records. Their baptisms, marriages and burials appear in the parish registers, but often this is all we know about them. Married women lost their identity. They could not carry on business, sue in a court of law or make a will without their husbands' permission, and everything they had belonged to him. But spinsters and widows could carry on a trade, sue in a court of law and dispose of their property as they wished by will and testament. Widows such as Alison Taylor, Agnes Palfreyman, Ellen and Margaret Harrison, and Isobel Woodward struggled to repossess the debts owed to their husbands. Between 1591-2 Margaret Harrison a widow sued John Nash and Thomas Sacheverell for debts owing to her dead husband, and Isobel Woodward pursued Thomas Sacheverell

and Anthony Bate through the courts for a debt of £10 owing to her husband when he died in 1595.

Trespass and assault were also common injuries brought before the Derby borough court at the end of the 16th century. Francis Morris the maltster of Sadlergate was involved in several such cases. In 1590 he was sued by Thomas Wright and Henry Fisher for trespass. In 1592 he in turn sued Lawrence Hodgkinson for trespass. After that date the incidents show an escalation in violence. In 1593 Francis Morris claimed damages against Ralph Morris for trespass, against William Sadler for trespass and assault, and John Sadler for trespass and insult. In 1594 Morris sued John Parker and Michael Beardsley for trespass and assault. In 1595 he sued Christopher Morris for trespass and assault, and in conjunction with his wife Marie sued William Botham for trespass. Between 1596-9 he was involved in a further 10 cases of trespass and assault including one against a tenant living in his house in Sadlergate, William Firebrace a shoemaker. Francis Morris sold this house in 1616 to John Parke of Castleton.[5]

This sorry catalogue of disputes between neighbours was not unusual in the 16th century, but minor incidents such as trespass were to pale into insignificance beside the events which were to overtake Derby, and the whole country in the mid-17th century.

Chapter Five

Civil War and Restoration— 17th-Century Derby

◆

The town was to get a new charter in 1611. This meant that it was to be governed by two bailiffs, 24 burgesses, a recorder or judge, a chamberlain to keep the town treasury, and a town clerk to oversee the day-to-day running of the town. The bailiffs were able to take their wine from two great standing cups with covers worth £23 6s. 8d. which were given to the town by Mr. Walton. He also gave the town a £100 interest-free loan to tide it over difficult times.

In 1637 the composition of the town council was changed again to one headed by a mayor, an upper house of nine aldermen, and a lower chamber of 14 brethren and 14 burgesses. The first mayor was Henry Mellor. Part of the function of the town council was to provide improving entertainment for the populace. Religious plays such as the play of *Holofernes* were performed by the 'townsmen' for the edification of the citizens. The townsmen were probably a group of players retained by the town.

In the 17th century the town was involved in events of national importance. Charles I was unpopular in Derby because of his high church brand of religion, and the unconstitutional taxes he levied. In 1626, when the inhabitants of the town were invited to give a 'free gift' which was an euphemism for an enforced loan to the king, they assembled before the bailiffs and stated that they refused to lend the king any money. Eventually 10 citizens gave £20 4s. 0d. among them, and the Justices of the Peace contributed a further £91. Despite this William Hutton, writing in the 18th century, noted a tradition that Charles I had stayed in the town in 1635, sleeping at a great house in the Market Place and receiving from the corporation livestock and a purse of gold to help with his catering arrangements. The corporation also gave money to the king's nephews, the Princes Maurice and Rupert of the Rhine, who were to become legendary as cavalry leaders in the Civil War.[1]

One of the most unpopular taxes was Ship Money which Charles demanded that towns and villages should pay to help finance the Navy. In August 1635 Derby was asked to pay £175 for 'the fitting out of a ship of war and for the levy of money for the expenses of its officers, men and munitions'.[2] This was a considerable amount for the town to find and increased the king's unpopularity. Parliament tried to check the king's excesses which led to a confrontation between the monarch and his government.

20 Gervaise Sleigh, an early 17th-century bailiff of the town.

In May 1641 Parliament mobilised its supporters. Charles raised his standard at Nottingham in August 1641, and sent out a muster order to all the Lords Lieutenant of the counties ordering them to send him troops. The Civil War had started. The event was noted in the All Saints' parish register which added that only 20 Derby men marched to join the king. This was out of a muster roll of 860 able-bodied men.

As Charles began his march westward Derby found itself in a vulnerable position because it housed the county magazine of arms. But although Charles and his troops were in the town for three days, the magazine was still intact when Sir John Gell, the Parliamentarian commander, established his headquarters in the town hall. Gell was joined by Sir George Gresley and other Parliamentarians. On 13 December 1642 they wrote to Speaker Lenthall in London that they had 700 men ready at Derby, but were in need of arms to defend the town against malignant royalists. The malignants came from the area surrounding the town and included Sir John Harpur of Calke Abbey and Sir John Fitzherbert. Supporters of Parliament included John Mundy of Markeaton and Robert Wilmot of Chaddesden.

Sir John Gell of Kirk Ireton has come down through history as an uncompromising and harsh man who was determined to get his own way. He used Derby as a base from which to attack the Royalist forces and it became the headquarters of the Parliamentarian Derby Committee. Gell was appointed governor of Derby by the Earl of Essex on 17 January 1642/3. In the same month the Derby committee sent out a notice to muster cavalry who were to gather at the house of Nathanial Hallam in Derby for training and exercises. A general call to arms was also sent out to defend the town against

21   Sir John Gell.

'divers papists, Robbers and other lewd persons who are come into country and are very nere the town of Derbie'. When no arms or men were forthcoming, the Derby Committee sent an impassioned plea to London asking for the requisition of a troop of horse to help to defend the town because 'a troop of horse led by a bloody and desperate malignant is quartered near the town—Colonel Hastings has boasted that he will put Gell out of Derby before Thursday next'.[3]

In spite of this threat Gell survived, and on 19 March 1643 was engaged with the Royalists at Hopton Heath outside Lichfield. Although the Royalist commander, the Earl of Northampton, was slain, the Parliamentarian forces lost the day, and Sir John Gell was forced to withdraw to Derby, bringing the body of the earl with him. Despite requests from the earl's family for its return, Gell had it dragged round the town before displaying it naked in the market place. Eventually it was thrown into the Cavendish vault in All Saints' Church.[4]

In 1644 Royalist agents from the Royalist stronghold at Bolsover infiltrated Derby. They tried to raise the townspeople against Parliament, but were discovered by the Parliamentarian troops and driven away. However, Gell's argumentative and overbearing ways were creating divisions within his own side. In 1643 there was a confrontation between Gell and Major Thomas Sanders over the replacement of the town recorder after the royalist recorder William Allestree had fled. Allestree's estates were seized by Parliament and a fine put on them. Gell wanted his own brother Thomas to have the office. Sanders preferred the Puritan, Exuperius Fletcher, who was commander of the Coleorton garrison, as a candidate. By coercion and intimidation Gell got his brother elected to the post.

22 Memorial to William Allestrey, the royalist recorder of Derby, in All Saints' Church.

Sanders and Gell were to clash again in 1645 over the nomination of the Member of Parliament for the town. Gell again wanted his brother to be nominated, but Sanders supported Robert Mellor. Gell exercised his superiority of command and removed Mellor from the scene by ordering him to garrison Chatsworth. Gell then set about intimidating the burgesses into choosing his candidate. On the day of the election he sat by the town hall noting the names of the burgesses as they came to vote. Despite Gell's grim presence, by midday it was clear that Mellor was in the lead, especially as the mayor, one of Mellor's supporters, had a letter signed by 60 absentees giving Mellor their vote. Mellor won the election by 149 to 70 votes, but two returns were sent to the High Sheriff of Derbyshire. One declared Mellor the winner, the other Thomas Gell. It was not until 1647 that the Parliamentary Committee of Privileges declared Gell to be the winner, thus indicating that Parliamentarian

power was as corrupt as that held previously by the crown.

The severity of Gell and his puritanical rule during the Commonwealth period alienated the town. On 11 August 1659 there was a rising in Sherwood Forest in favour of Charles II. The following day a Colonel White proclaimed Charles as king in Derby market place. Traders closed their shops and whilst some townsfolk declared for a restored monarchy others stood by a free parliament. Colonel White was arrested by Colonel Sanders but escaped, and Sanders himself was forced to flee from the town to General Lambert, who returned with his troops. Their overwhelming weight of numbers persuaded the Royalists to withdraw quietly and the incident ended without bloodshed.

The eventual restoration of the Stuart monarchy was viewed with relief in the town. Bells were rung in the parish churches and the new king Charles II was once again proclaimed in the market place.

On the eve of the Civil War, Derby had affirmed its belief in the Protestant religion by sending a petition to the king asking him 'to maintain the Power and Purity of the Protestant religion'.[5] During the war the Protestants had divided into many different sects. In 1650 the leader of one of these, George Fox of the Society of Friends or Quakers, was imprisoned in Derby for nearly a year. There is a tradition that the name Quaker was applied to the Society of Friends in Fox's trial at Derby and it is true that it was during his sojourn in Derby that Fox referred in his journal to the Society as Quakers. He writes that Justice Bennet of Derby 'was the first that called us Quakers, because we bid them tremble at the word of the Lord'.

Fox recounts in his journal what happened to him in Derby. Hearing that a great lecture was to be given in All Saints' Church by a colonel in the army, which officers of the army, priests and preachers were to attend, he felt compelled to go, and when the preacher had done to say to them 'what the Lord commanded me, and they were pretty quiet'. He was summarily arrested and brought before the magistrates Gervaise Bennet, and Nathaniel Barton who had given the lecture. After an interrogation and angry disputation that lasted for seven hours, Fox was sentenced to six months' imprisonment in the House of Correction.

Fox wrote to the justices, priests, the mayor of Derby, the Court and the 'ringers who used to ring the bells in the steeple-house, called St Peter's, in Derby' that: 'I am moved to write unto you, to take heed of oppressing the poor in your Courts, or laying burthens upon poor people, which they cannot bear; and of imposing false oaths, or making them take oaths which they cannot perform ...'. He exhorts them to have mercy as 'the Lord delighteth in mercy'.

Whilst Fox was in the House of Correction his relatives offered to be bound in one hundred pounds that if he were freed he would come no more to Derby and declare against priests. But he would not consent to this and, whilst he was praying for God's forgiveness for the justices who had committed him, 'Justice Bennet rose up in a rage ... and struck me with both his hands'.

Near the end of his imprisonment in the House of Correction Fox was taken out to the market place and before the soldiers and the commissioners of the Derby committee was asked whether he would take up arms and a command in the Commonwealth army. When he refused he was taken away and put in the common gaol, 'a lousy, stinking place, low in the ground, without any bed, amongst thirty felons'. He was to remain there for another six months. However, Fox thought that God had wrought revenge on the town for its treatment of him as 'the waters ran from the town dam when the flood-gates were up'. Eventually he was released at the beginning of the winter in the year 1651. In that year another Quaker, Elizabeth Hooton, was also imprisoned for interrupting a service in All Saints' Church.[6]

The Presbyterians, a group which were against church government by bishops, also had supporters in Derby. In 1665 a government informer, Thomas Caulton accused a group of Presbyterians in the East Midlands of plotting an uprising against the crown. In the panic that followed this all known Presbyterians in Derbyshire were rounded up and brought to Derby for questioning. Five were thrown into gaol: Philip Wild, Francis Shelby, James Wright, John How and Robert Hollingworth. However, only Philip Wild was prosecuted, and he was pardoned by the king and released in 1667. The Presbyterians continued to prosper in Derby and in 1698 built a handsome chapel in Friargate. This was demolished in 1974.

23 The Friends Meeting House in the early 19th century.

24 The Friargate Chapel in the late 19th century.

25 John Flamsteed the first Astronomer-Royal, who was born in Denby and educated in Derby.

In 1677 a return made by clergymen about the religious faith of their parishioners shows that in All Saints' and St Alkmund's there were 1,113 communicants in the Anglican church, four papists and 49 non-conformists. In St Peter's parish there were 500 members of the Church of England, 40 non-conformists but no papists, St Michael's parish had 63 members of the Church of England but no dissenters, and in St Werburgh's there were 338 communicants and no Catholics or non-conformists.

Although the town had welcomed the return of the Stuarts it watched their flirtation with Catholic faith with apprehension. In 1678 there was panic when a rumour started that the papists were to gather on Nuns' Green and take the town.

Ten years later a group of Protestant noblemen led by the Earl of Devonshire were to force the abdication of the Catholic king James II, and invite the Protestant sovereigns William and Mary to take the throne. The bloodless 'Glorious Revolution' of 1688 was engineered from Derbyshire. The group of confederates who arranged this met at the 'Revolution House' near Chesterfield, whilst the Earl of Devonshire stayed at Derby during the negotiations. On 20 November 1688 the earl delivered an address to the mayor and corporation of the town which explained the confederates' intentions. He then rode to Nottingham to declare these openly, knowing that he had the support of his own county town behind him.

In 1646 John Flamsteed was born in Denby in Derbyshire. He was educated at the Free School in Derby, and later taught himself astronomy. Isaac Newton became his patron, and helped him to get

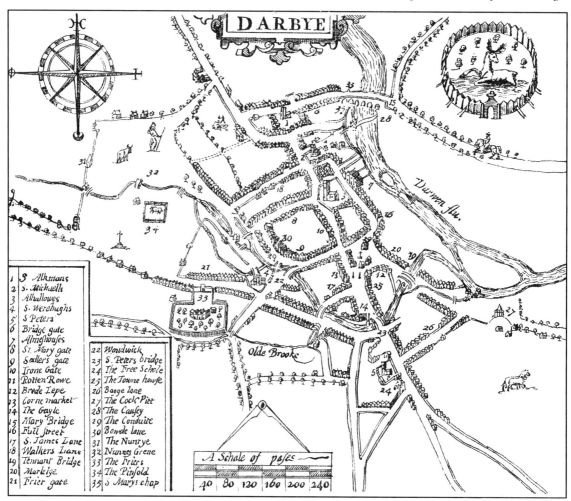

26   John Speed's map of Derby, 1610.

into the University of Cambridge. Later, however, the two men fell out and there was an unseemly altercation between them at a meeting of the Royal Society. Flamsteed's first published observation was on the solar eclipse that took place on 25 October 1668.

Flamsteed eventually took holy orders, and after a short period in a living in Derbyshire moved south. He was appointed as the first Astronomer Royal in 1675. He died in 1719 and was buried in the parish church of Burstow in Surrey.

At the end of the 17th century the population of the town amounted to about 3,000 souls living in 604 households. Eighty of these households were the homes of pauper families such as that of Thomas Creavey, described as a 'poor old man'. The houses the poor lived in often had only one or two rooms with a central hearth for heating and cooking. But 70 per cent of Derby's citizens lived in substantial houses with at least two hearths. Some had very large houses boasting at least 10 hearths, such as Henry More's dwelling in All Saints' parish, or that of Sir John Shore with 18 hearths.[7]

In the centre of the town shops or other retail outlets were incorporated into the houses as this description of a dwelling in the Cornmarket known as the Horse and Trumpet shows. This complex of buildings had a kitchen, passage room, buttery and a large shop front. There was a cellar beneath the shop and rooms above the shop and kitchen. The whole was enclosed within its own yard guarded by a gatehouse and covered passage, both with rooms above them. In the yard was a large building used by William Wragg as a malt mill, a pig stye, a place to lay coals and tie beasts lay under a hovel used by Isaac Hegge to lay kids (faggots), gorse and other baker's fuel. Also in the yard was a midden hole and a place of office or toilet.

More modest was Luke Nield's barber's shop in Babington Lane for which he paid 40s. a year, or the cottage on the Morledge where Nathaniel Columbell, a labourer, lived in three rooms, two downstairs and one above, for which he paid 20s. a year.[8]

Most houses in late 17th-century Derby were well built of brick, and the town had an air of bustle about it, as in this description left by Celia Fiennes when she visited the town in 1698:

Darby town lies down in a bottom built all of brick or for the most part, there are 5 Churches built of

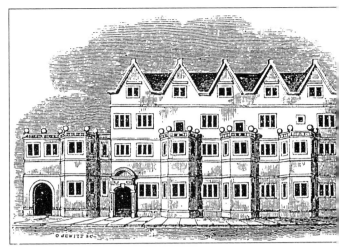

27 Mr. Jessopp's house, Wardwick is now known as the Jacobean House.

stone the biggest of which I was in, the tower was finely carv'd full of niches and pedistals whereon statues had been set, but nothing worth notice in the inside except a monument over the vault of the Duke of Devonshire, on which stands 2 effigies at length all of white marble the Earle and his Countess of Devonshire with an arch or cannopy of stone over their heads, this is rail's in with iron grates, there is also another statue gilded lying at length which is also rail'd in; the River Derwent runs by the town and turns many mills and the water engine which turns the water into the pipes that serves the town, the same wheele grinds also, but they do it for a half penny a strike which is the same measure as our bushell, at this Engine they can grind if its never so high a flood which hinders all the others from working, at the flood they are quite choaked up, but this they can set higher or lower just as the water is; there are bay's which they make with stones to keep the water to run to the mill and thence it falls againe into the Derwent; there is also a fine stone Cunduite in the Market place which is very spacious well pitch'd, a good

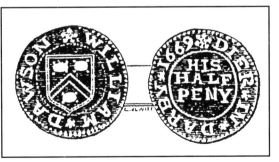

28   In the 17th century traders issued their own currency known as traders' tokens. This is a 19th-century drawing of trade token from Derby.

29   The Derwent from St Mary's Bridge.

Market Cross; this is a dear place for strangers notwithstanding the plentyfullness of all provision my dinner cost me 5s and 8d., only 2 servant men with me and I had but a shoulder of mutton and bread and beer; here they make great quantetys of gloves. I did not observe or learn any other trade or manufacture, they had only shops and all sorts of things; they carry much of their carriages on sledges to secure their pitching in the streets.[9]

Celia Fiennes was most impressed by the conduit and compared it favourably with others she saw on her travels. It had been constructed in 1692 by George Sorocold who had leased the land and

mills in order to develop a water works from the corporation in 1691. The water was transported by a network of wooden pipes and the engine described by Celia Fiennes pumped the water to conduits situated in the Market Place and Babington Lane.

The town Celia Fiennes saw, which had retailing as its prime function, was changing. Very soon Derby was to have the first operational textile mill in Great Britain, and would lead the country into changes in manufacturing processes that would alter patterns of life and labour forever.

Chapter Six

Silk, China, Society and Rebels— Derby in the Early 18th Century

In the early 18th century Derby was noted for its malt houses and the good ale it produced. In 1712 William Woolley noted malting as being the town's principal trade, with malt being sent as far afield as Lancashire. He added that the town was famous for 'very good ale which the brewers send to London and other parts to good advantage'. Woolley was also impressed by the market place, 'On the East side of the Market stands a handsome large pile of building called the Court, which helps to grace it

much, as does the Cross, under which there is a good conduit of water brought out of Newlands ...'.[1]

When Daniel Defoe visited the town in 1725 he described it as a 'town of gentry rather than of trade yet it is populous, well built, has five parishes a large market place, a fine town house, and very handsome streets'. However, as shown in Domesday Book and the town's first charter which granted the burgesses a monopoly in working dyed cloth, there had been a cloth industry in the town since the medieval period, and it was this area of trade which was to develop into the first industrial mill, not only in Derby but the whole country.[2]

Before the mills and factories of the Industrial Revolution, thread and textiles were produced by domestic workers in their own homes. Producing the thread which was to be woven into cloth or knitted into stockings was a lengthy process, and for many years a way was sought to speed this up and to produce a greater quantity of thread at a cheaper price. The Italian silk industry was in the forefront of this research, and it was to Italy that a London merchant with Derby connections, Thomas Lombe, went to search for a spinning machine. He found what he was looking for in Piedmont. It was an engine which would wind, spin and twist raw silk ready to be handed to the weavers or knitters to be converted into finished goods. In 1718 George I granted Thomas Lombe a patent to put these engines into operation in a mill situated in Derby. In the same year Thomas Cheshire of London, a silk throwster, and Francis Cockayne also of London, a silkman, leased an orchard and summer house in Babington Lane for £4 10s. a year, suggesting that Derby was already noted for its silk workers and products. This was one of the reasons that the town

30 Title page of an early newspaper printed in Derby showing the deer in the park.

was chosen by Lombe for his experimental machinery, but it was also chosen partly because of Lombe's connections with the town, and partly because it was at the centre of the framework knitting industry which would use the silk thread produced by the engines.

The Lombe family had been in Derby for many generations. They appear in town records from the 16th century onwards. A relation of Thomas Lombe, John Lombe was already an experienced silk manufacturer who had worked to produce silk in a mill which had been set up by Thomas Cotchett in 1702.

Thomas Cotchett was a solicitor, born in Mickleover in 1640. He diversified his interests into the production of silk yarn, no doubt perceiving the growing demand for this product by the stocking knitters. Unfortunately Cotchett's ideas were ahead of his time, and he had neither the expertise nor the machinery available to make a success of his venture. It is thought that Cotchett had a mill driven by water power which was on the site or next door to the mill that the Lombes set up. The Lombes asked George Sorocold to design the mill and its engineering for them.

The mill lay beside the Derwent on By Flat next to corn and saw mills, all of which were using power from the river. The Lombes' mill was powered by water controlled by two sluices and run by an undershot wheel. This was a type of water wheel which stood in the water and was moved by the force of the current. Defoe was fascinated by the mill but had doubts as to whether it answered the expense of its erection. He recounts a story about

32 19th-century photograph of a Derby mill with water wheel.

Sorocold who fell into the river when showing some visitors the water wheel and was caught between two of its paddles. The wheel came to a halt, but one of the paddles broke under the pressure and Sorocold was spewed forth onto dry land 'like Jonah's whale'.[3]

One who experienced life in the mill at first hand was William Hutton, who at the age of seven was placed in a seven-year apprenticeship in the mill. He described these years as the most unhappy years of his life. In later life he recalled that as he was too small to reach the machines heavy metal pattens were fastened to his feet which he was forced to drag around. He wrote, 'the confinement and the labour were no hardship, but the severity was intolerable, the marks of which I shall carry to the grave'. He gives a harrowing account of being hoisted onto the back of 'Bryan Barker, a giant of approaching seven feet being like hoisted onto the back of a precipice, where the wicked instrument of affliction was wielded with pleasure; but alas it was only a pleasure to one side'. Hutton quotes a rumour current in Derby during his childhood that John Lombe was poisoned by Italians angry at loosing their secret.[4]

Part of Lombes' mill was burned down in 1826, and the whole was remodelled in the 1830s. Today, Derby Industrial Museum is housed in the mill buildings. Its Italian-style tower provides a landmark that draws the eye to the impressive multi-storey red-brick building. In the 18th and 19th centuries this was a prestige building entered through a pair of magnificent wrought-iron gates made by the master iron worker Robert Bakewell.

31   19th-century view of the Old Silk Mill.

The success of the mill was to turn Derby into one of the foremost silk throwing towns in the country; supplying silk thread for a multitude of uses. In 1777 there were at least eight silk mills in the town. On 21 October of that year eight mill owners placed a notice in the *Derby Mercury* stating that they had formed an association of silk throwsters to apprehend persons stealing silk or silk waste. By 1789 there were 12 mills in the town. Other factories made the silk into ribbons, and the town was noted for these in the late 18th and early 19th centuries.

In the 18th century the livelihood of at least 18 per cent of the total population was connected with silk trade. This included many women and children. The silk industry was equally as important in the 19th century, and a recession in the textile trade during the 1830s caused hardship to a great number of the town's folk. In an attempt to improve conditions and wages, workers joined trade unions which had been legalised in the Combination Acts of 1824-5. These acts recognised combinations of workmen and their right to collect funds providing there was no coercion involved, but the Acts also made the unions subject to the common law which dealt with conspiracy and coercion. Any trade unionist found guilty of these through union action would be deemed a felon and could be imprisoned, transported or, in extreme cases, executed.

The dispute in the silk industry in Derby started in November 1833 when a silk throwster, Mr. Foster, discharged a workman who refused to pay a fine for an infringement of mill regulations. His fellow workers walked out in support of him, and at the end of the first week of the strike there were 800 workers on strike in the town. Although the strike had been sparked off by one small incident, it was connected to the wider issue of the silk workers' wish to be allowed to join a trade union without being dismissed.

The employers met at the *Kings Head* to discuss this aspect, and as a result of this meeting issued a statement to the effect that they recognised the right of work people to combine, but objected to the secret oaths taken by trade unions, and therefore declined to employ trade union members. This statement was signed by 20 employers and it amounted to an exclusion of union members from the silk mills of the town. The strike had become a lock out.

By 4 December 1833 there were 1,300 workers locked out. In order to maintain public order the corporation enrolled special constables and the dragoons from Nottingham were held on stand-by.

On 15 January 1834 the mills advertised for non-union labour, and by 14 February, although there were 2,000 workers affected by the lock out, some mills had started work again. There were cases of intimidation by union members trying to prevent 'black legs' from working. Those charged with intimidation included women as well as men. For example, Mary Cooper and Ruth Beeston were sentenced to three months' imprisonment for intimidation and violence against Ann Glover, and 'females' Fearn and Radford were bound over to keep the peace and to desist from insulting women coming out of the silk mills at the end of their shifts.

In February 1834 Robert Owen, the radical reformer who had mills of his own at New Lanark, had formed the Grand National Consolidated Trade Union which was to include all workers regardless of gender or age. Owen himself visited Derby during the lock out, but as a neutral conciliator rather than a supporter of the workers. A Derby Committee of the Grand National was set up in Birmingham which took practical steps to get the workers back to work by offering to buy silk machinery from the employers and run its own mill. This offer was rejected by the employers, and more non-union labour was recruited to run the mills. The employers felt that not only were they in the right but were also amongst the righteous when the Rev. Thomas Gisburne, Prebendary of Durham Cathedral but born in Derby, preached a sermon which urged all workers to give up trade unions as being against the scriptures.

33 The Old China works in Nottingham Road.

Those who remained locked out were living on 7s. a week strike pay from their unions, but funds were depleted and by March 1834 many faced starvation and were compelled by hunger to renounce their principles and return to work. Gradually the dispute faded out, and by June 1834 all silk mills were in production again. It had been a hard and bitter six months for the town. Nevertheless the silk industry remained a staple of the town until foreign competition in the late 19th century reduced production, and only two silk mills survived into the 20th century.[5]

The other industry which developed in the 18th century for which Derby is justly proud is the production of fine porcelain. The Derby China Factory was opened in 1750 by André Planché, a Huguenot refugee, and William Duesbury, who moved

34 *(left)*   The Kedleston Vase, *c.*1790. The painting on a salmon ground is by Zachariah Boreman, on the reverse is a painting of 'Virgins awakening Cupid' by Banford with a swag of roses by Billingsley.

35 *(above)*   Shell-shaped dish with thistle painting by W. Pegg, *c.*1813.

to Derby from Longton in the Staffordshire potteries. Duesbury was the business man and Planché the artist who specialised in the production of porcelain figures, and the early work of the factory is characterised by figures and small fine objects such as cream jugs and sauce boats with a white or cream glaze.

The works was put on a more commercial footing in 1756 by an agreement between Duesbury, Planché and John Heath, a local banker. This period marks the introduction of more functional ware to the range, such as tea pots and coffee jugs decorated in a Chinese style with figures in pale colours and pale gilding.

In 1764 Duesbury purchased the bankrupt Chelsea pottery in London, and used the expertise there to produce a better quality ware at Derby which was decorated with classical and pastoral subjects in clear bright colours. Also at this time a popular range of figures illustrating contemporary worthies and characters from the past appeared. These included Shakespeare, John Milton and a series of actors including David Garrick and Edmund Kean playing Richard III.

When William Duesbury died in 1786 his son, another William, took over. The works began to concentrate on tableware with landscapes painted on to the china. These included local landscapes as well as imaginary scenes. When the Chelsea works closed for good the best workers moved to Derby. Two of these, Zachariah Boreman and Thomas Hills, produced characteristic straight-sided coffee cups in canary yellow. Another artist, William Billingsley, specialised in decorating the porcelain with flower paintings. In about 1790 these artists were joined by J.S. Spangler, a Swiss potter who specialised in figures in a Romantic style. Seascapes and naval battles also became popular motifs at this time. The colours on the porcelain became opaque and the glaze harder in this period.

At the beginning of the 19th century the paintings of fruit and flower became naturalistic. Two notable flower painters were John Brewer and William Pegg, 'the Quaker', whilst Thomas Steele produced designs of fruit on flat panels. In about 1815 birds were added to the range of decoration, and until 1825 were the work of Richard Dodson. There was also a revival of interest in figures in the

1820s. Animals and children were the most popular subjects.

The earliest works were in Nottingham Road by St Mary's Bridge. They remained there until 1790 when they moved to an enlarged works, also situated in Nottingham Road. In 1848 the Nottingham Road works were closed and the workmen thrown out of work. A group of them pooled their savings and set up their own works in King Street. It is just possible to make out the sign advertising these premises above the Mountain Sports Shop opposite to St Helen's House.

The expertise of Derby's porcelain painters was not forgotten by those dealing in china. In 1865 Edward Phillips and Richard Binns purchased land near the Arboretum with the hope of starting a second china works in the town. However, they could not afford to build the works until a consortium of businessmen was formed which included Edward Litherland, a Liverpool retailer of china, and the local printer, William Bemrose, who had helped to promote the works locally.

In 1875 the Derby Crown Porcelain Company was opened in Osmaston Road. Queen Victoria granted the company the right to add Royal to their title in 1890. Meanwhile the King Street works had continued to produce good quality china, and it was not until 1935 that the two works combined. In 1964 the Royal Crown Derby P.C. became part of the Allied Potteries Group.[6]

Other trades in early 18th-century Derby reflect changing fashions in building. The large houses built along Friargate had elaborate plaster work inside, which was often the work of George Monypenny of Little Chester. Unlike earlier buildings in the town these were constructed of stone or brick with tiled roofs. The trades of plasterer, tiler and bricklayer start to appear in the Derby records during the early years of the 18th century. Valentine the younger, William and Samuel Francis, and Robert and John Simpson were all plasterers who lived on the Morledge. Robert Simpson's house adjoined the Bowling Green and had a frontage of 63 ft. He paid 40s. a year for this which suggests that he earned a good wage. Samuel Francis and John Simpson paid 20s. a year for their smaller houses which had frontages of 15 ft. and consisted of one downstairs room and two chambers above. Larger houses were found in the Cornmarket. The rent on

36   Linsmore vase attributed to John Brewer 1812-15.

37 New china works, engraving taken from a photograph by W. Winter.

these was as much as £7 a year. This rent was paid by Sarah Bancroft for her dwelling on which she had a seven-year lease. Her near neighbour was Henry Every, a tallow chandler.[7]

Tallow chandlery was a notoriously smelly business as the main ingredient of the tallow was the rendered down carcase of an animal that had been allowed to decay, so the Cornmarket was not a salubrious place in the 18th century. The brook that crossed it was nothing more than an open sewer and it was above this that the county gaol was situated, where the inhabitants were not only exposed to the foul stench, danger of death by drowning or disease but were also in full view of the passers-by. The prisoners, many of whom were in prison for debt, lived on bread and river water and slept on plank beds. In 1724 Thomas Litchfield, who had a house which backed onto the gaol, created a causeway which diverted the watercourse used to 'cleanse and scour the filth and nastiness from the Gaol' and created even worse conditions inside the prison. The Quarter Sessions records of 1732 show that there was a female keeper of the gaol in that year, a Mrs. Mary Greatorex. She was asked at this session how she meant to recapture three escaped prisoners, Elias Wheldon, George Hamblet and John Bradshaw.

Escape from the gaol was all too easy. A window that overlooked the Cornmarket was one escape route, but the determined prisoner could break down the walls and get out on to the bridge that crossed the brook. In 1752 four prisoners did this. One returned by the same route the next morning, but the other three were never seen again.

One unhappy prisoner in the gaol was Eleanor Beare, whose career was narrated by William Hutton who, at the age of eight, was an eye witness to some of the events. Eleanor Beare was the landlady of the *White Horse* inn. In 1732 she was a handsome woman of about thirty years. She was married, but Hutton describes her husband Ebenezer as a mere cipher. He writes 'She (Eleanor) was remarkably expert at procuring qualifications for men; an exit for those women who were troublesome wives; and abortions for those who were not'. One man who had a troublesome wife was John Hewit of Stepping Lane. His cruelty and neglect of his wife was such that she sought relief in alcohol and was often intoxicated. Hewit and his wife frequented the *White Horse*, and it was not long before Hewit was not only Eleanor Beare's lover, but also the lover of her maidservant Rosamund Ollerenshaw. To Eleanor the affair was a mere dalliance, but Rosamund wanted to marry Hewit, and he felt the same about her. Accordingly they conspired to murder Mrs. Hewit by putting arsenic into some pancake batter which Eleanor Beare had made for her. Mrs. Hewit died three hours after eating the pancakes, and Hewit, Eleanor and Rosamund were accused of her murder.

Hewit tried to throw all the blame onto Eleanor, but under cross-examination Rosamund told the truth, that Eleanor had no knowledge of the poison, but had made the batter and left it, and she had added the poison. She cleared Eleanor but condemned herself and her lover. Hewit and Rosamund were executed together. Hewit who seems to have been truly fond of Rosamund supporting her on the scaffold as she was unable to stand.

Eleanor Beare was charged at the next Assizes with entering into a compact with a young man to get rid of his wife, and of receiving five guineas to secure an abortion for a Nottingham lady by the insertion of an instrument resembling an iron skewer. She was found guilty and sentenced to three years' imprisonment, and to stand in the pillory in the Market Place on two occasions, where Hutton saw her on 18 August 1732 covered with excrement and rotting vegetable matter. The pillory being in poor repair she escaped and ran down the Morledge,

38 The old *White Horse Inn*.

a moving heap of ordure. Recaptured she was returned to the pillory with difficulty where Hutton saw 'the exasperated brother of the unfortunate Rosamund pull her with violence into the pillory by her hair ... Her punishment exceeded death. By the time they had fixed her, the hours had expired and she was carried back to prison, an object which none cared to touch'.

The next Friday she was pilloried again. She appeared not as a young woman 'but an old one, ill, swelled and decrepid. She seemed to have aged thirty years in one week.' Hutton adds that when she was released from prison three years later she had regained her health, ripeness and beauty and was met by a triumphant band of musicians.[8]

The sorry and insanitary condition of the gaol induced the county authorities to build a plain but substantial prison in Friargate which was opened in 1756, and could house felons and debtors separately. It also included a House of Correction for short sharp shocks. It was designed by Mr. Irons of Warwick. It had a governor's house and three exercise yards, one for male felons, one for male debtors and inmates of the House of Correction, and one for female prisoners. Seven separate cells kept the worst

39 Punishment in the pillory. Illustration from an 18th-century chap-book.

offenders from the rest, but the other prisoners lived, ate and slept in a common room, unless they had funds, when the governor could rent them the use of two rooms above the chapel or an apartment in his house. Felons were put in irons for their trial, and aggressive or refractory prisoners were put into shackles and chained to the wall at the discretion of the governor. When there was work available the prisoners were required to comb wool, or dress flax. If they had money the prisoners could buy food and drink; if not, they lived on bread and water.

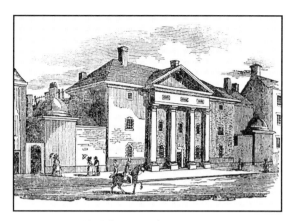

40 The new gaol in Friargate.

Debtors were allowed to walk on the prison roof and for 6d. a week could have the privilege of having sheets and a flock mattress on their beds. Designed to house 21 felons and 26 debtors the county gaol was soon massively overcrowded and conditions inside became as bad as those in the old gaol in the Cornmarket. In order to ameliorate these a bathroom was added, and the prison walls were scraped free of filth and whitewashed every year.

The County Hall where the Assizes met had been rebuilt in 1660, after the Grand Jurors had presented a petition to the judges stating their dissatisfaction with the existing hall as being remote from the prison, convenient inns and lodgings. William Hutton writing in the late 18th century suggests that the master mason in charge of the work drank away his profits, whilst the carpenter Roger Morledge syphoned off timber for use on his own house in St Helen's Walk.

The new county hall opened in 1697 with Richard Leach as its first keeper. His tasks were to maintain the gardens surrounding the hall, and to lay out the cushions for the Grand Assizes. However, he was reported to have turned the Jury Room into an ale house, and set up nine pins in the garden. He was dismissed in 1709 but allowed to keep the garden. This was laid out in a formal style with rows of pollarded limes. These had disappeared by the time Hutton published his book in 1791.

In 1763 the gateway to the court was widened to admit coaches, and in 1808 the *Marlborough Head* public house was purchased and judges lodgings erected on the site. When the Assizes were not sitting the courtyard in front of the hall was used for a variety of purposes including a gymnasium where fencers could practice sword play, and bearwards, dancers and 'loose idle disorderly persons' all used the court's grounds. In 1730 Isaac Borrow the mayor who lived in St Mary's Gate was allowed to store his new sash windows in the courtyard, and in 1743 the organ builder installing the new organ in All Saints church was given permission to assemble the parts in the county hall.[9]

The growth of the town in the early 18th century meant more demand for produce. Leases show that market gardens could be found inside the town. One in St Peter's parish was leased by Charles Purslove for £4 10s. a year. Derbyshire cheese was also becoming a well known commodity in the 18th century. In 1734 Derby added a cheese market to its other markets, and from here Derbyshire cheese, including the famous Sage Derby, was sent all over the country. Rolling and slitting mills on the Morledge for smelting iron shows that heavy industry was moving into the town and changing it from the gentry town described by Defoe to an industrial centre.

Life was not all work in 18th-century Derby. In 1732 the town's population gathered to watch a high wire artiste slide down a wire suspended between the two church towers of All Saints' and St Michael's. Such was the velocity of the descent that it was reported that smoke was seen issuing from the rope. When the virtuoso tried to repeat the performance at Shrewsbury he fell off the rope and was killed.

In 1714 Assembly Rooms were opened for the entertainment of the gentry and wealthier members of society. These rooms were run by strict etiquette which forbade shopkeepers and tradesmen to enter the rooms. Rules were drawn up by the Ladies Assembly which not only barred shopkeepers and their families, but also attorneys' clerks. Ladies were not allowed to dance if wearing a long white apron or in coats, and there was a fine levied on those wearing mantuas. The Ladies Assembly was presided over by a mistress of ceremonies, Mrs. Anne Barnes, who was known by the nickname 'Blowzabella'. Scandal was to hit Mrs. Barnes in 1752 when it was found that she had exhausted the funds and had not kept up to date accounts. She was dismissed and Countess Ferrers took over the running of the rooms.

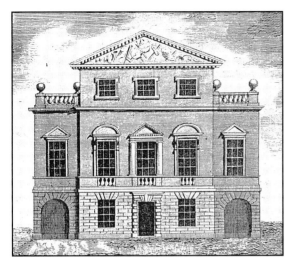

41   The Assembly Rooms in 1791.

The Assembly Rooms were rebuilt by public subscription between 1763-74. Joseph Pickford worked on these rooms, probably translating into practical terms a design drawn up by Earl Ferrers. The result was a handsome building of stone. On the instigation of Lord Scarsdale the interior was finished by Robert Adam in an elegant and restrained classical style. The accommodation inside included an elegant chandelier lit ball room, a card room and a room for taking tea. The interior of the building was gutted by fire in 1963 and demolished, although the frontage was removed to the Crich Tramway Museum where it can still be seen.

Another place of entertainment which opened in the 18th century was the theatre in Bold Lane. The first permanent theatre in the town. However, travelling players visited the town in 1713, and set

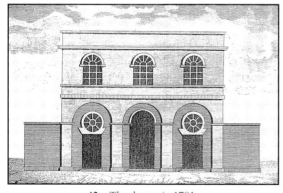

42   The theatre in 1791.

up their stage in the courtyard of County Hall. They were required to pay an indemnity against damage and give the court officials and their families free seats for the play. Other entertainment included an exhibition of 'Twenty Wild Beasts and Birds, All Alive' at the *White Lion Inn* in 1790. The animals which included a Bengal tiger were advertised for sale at the end of their time in Derby.[10]

Although most of the inhabitants of Derby supported the Protestant Hanoverian kings and the town returned Whig members to Parliament, the county was Tory and there were some in the town who still hankered after the old religion and the return of the Stuarts. In 1709 the assize chaplain, Dr. Henry Sacheverell preached a sermon in All Saints' which condemned the 'Glorious Revolution' of 1688. He was impeached for this, to the great rejoicing of the town.

In 1715 when the son of James II, Prince James Edward, known as the Old Pretender made a bid for the throne there were those in the town who supported him. The Rev. Samuel Sturges of All Saints' ill-advisedly prayed for King James in the church. A riot followed during which the Rev. Sturges was ushered from the pulpit at sword point. Tradition says that he never returned, but in fact he remained at his post until 1719 when he was succeeded by Dr. Michael Hutchinson. The Rev. Dr. Cantrill of St Alkmund's was reported to have Jacobite sympathies, and had been known to drink the Pretender's health. In the county Nicholas Leake, Earl of Scarsdale was a known Jacobite supporter, and in a by-election of 1742 another gentleman with Jacobite sympathies, German Pole was only narrowly defeated by the Whig candidate Henry Cavendish. Pole's party claimed that the Whig corporation of Derby had manipulated the result by creating a number of extra freemen who voted for the Whigs.

In 1745 Prince Charles Edward, the son of the Old Pretender landed in Scotland and marched south in a bid to claim the throne. The prelude to the invasion was a Declaration issued on 23 December 1743 by 'James III' asking for support for his 'Dearest Son The Prince of Wales' and claiming that he wanted to free the country from tyranny, heavy taxes, the calamities of war, the drainage of resources into German dominions, bribery and corruption, and the decay of trade and industry. He promised good behaviour on the part of his foreign invasion troops, and payment for military service for all those joining the Prince's army.

On 28 September 1745 the Duke of Devonshire as Lord Lieutenant of the county met with other gentlemen to discuss what they should do if the rebels were to reach Derby. At a further meeting on 3 October it was decided to raise a militia of 600 men under the command of the Marquess of Hartington the Duke's eldest son, and Sir Nathaniel Curzon of Kedleston. Privates in the militia were to be paid 1s. a day whilst in arms, and captains 8s. a day. A subscription list to support the militia was opened. It stated that voluntary

the rebels was at Ashbourne, and by 11 o'clock on that day they were entering Derby where they made their way to the *George Inn* where the magistrates were in session, and demanded billets for 9,000 men. The militia prudently withdrew to Nottingham.

The vanguard of the rebels wearing blue, red and gold then drew up in formation in the market place to await the prince and the main army. The town's folk, badly outnumbered rang bells in the prince's honour and lit bonfires to welcome him.

At about three in the afternoon Lord Elcho and the Lifeguards arrived in the town, followed by the main army marching six to eight abreast under

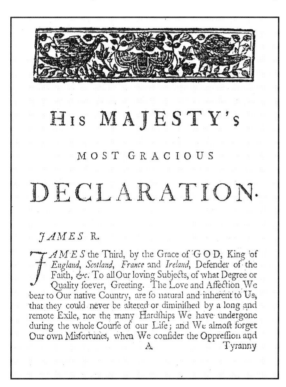

43   The title page of 'James III's' declaration asking for support for his son's invasion.

44   Prince Charles Edward Stuart as a young man.

subscriptions were required because 'a most wicked and unnatural Rebellion is begun against our rightfull Sovereign King George in order to subvert our Religion & Liberties ...'.

Meanwhile Prince Charles continued on his way southwards. He took Carlisle and marched through the Catholic north west gathering support as he went. He crossed the Mersey and set out towards the Trent. By 28 November 1745 the vanguard of

eight standards bearing the Crosses of St Andrew and St George, and accompanied by the swirl of the pipes. Despite their brave trappings the main army was a miserable sight, shabby and tired, a mixture of the able bodied, old men and boys scarce able to carry a pike who excited the town's folk's pity rather than their fear.

The Prince walked into town with the main army, and was proclaimed as king in the market place

45   Exeter House where Prince Charles stayed during his occupation of Derby.

by the town crier. He then went to lodge in Exeter House on the east bank of the Derwent, whilst the rest of the rebels crammed into private accommodation.

The next morning the rebels went shopping and sight seeing, much as any normal tourists might have done. However, the more unruly elements were accused of taking the goods they wanted without payment. The longer they stayed in the town the more undisciplined they became; they broke into gentlemen's houses to steal arms and generally upset the placid tenor of life.

What was the attitude of the town to the Prince? Accounts published shortly after the rebels stay in Derby which claim to give a true account of the conduct and proceedings of the rebels are at pains to show a town frightened by the numbers and fierceness of the rebels, especially the Hussars who were a 'parcel of fierce and desperate ruffians'. The townspeople, although unable to defend themselves, nevertheless steadfastly refused to take

up the offer of 5s. in advance if they joined the Prince and five guineas when they reached London. The rebels' sergeants desperately tried to drum up support for the Prince, and perhaps one of the reasons that the rebel army had made for Derby was because they thought that there was popular support for them in the town. However, only four Derby men enlisted in the Prince's army. Humphrey Cook, a blacksmith, stayed with the army as far as Culloden and was taken prisoner after the battle. Edward Hewit, a butcher, was also taken prisoner at Culloden, but died soon afterwards, probably from his wounds. James Sparkes, a framework knitter, was taken prisoner and executed on 26 October 1746. Charles Webster of Derby was also taken prisoner, tried for treason but acquitted of being a rebel.

Those citizens who had subscribed to the militia fund were forced to pay the same amount to the rebels, and all those owing excise duty were required to pay this to the rebels at the *Virgin Inn*, or face military execution. The extortion of excise money not only helped to swell the rebels' coffers, but it also helped to legitimise their cause as collecting the duty was the legal prerogative of the government, and thus if it was paid to the rebels it appeared as if they constituted the legal government of the country.

The post office was asked for a voluntary donation of £100 to the rebels, which was later commuted to £50. When this was not paid the postal clerk was threatened with murder, but escaped by jumping out of a window and fleeing for his life. Tales of theft, vandalism and brutality were recorded, and after the rebels had gone it was claimed that the houses they had inhabited looked like stables or pigsties.

Apart from the vain hope of popular support in the town why had the Prince made for Derby in the first place? It was well placed strategically, being in the centre of England and commanding the vital crossing of the Trent at Swarkestone Bridge, which the rebels quickly commandeered. It is also likely that they hoped for practical support from the Earl of Scarsdale, whilst an agent's report to Louis XIV of France suggested that John Manners, Duke of Rutland, Lord Chesterfield and Sir Nathaniel Curzon of Kedleston who were all local gentlemen would also support the Prince. As the latter was one of the commanders of the voluntary militia raised to defend the country against the rebels this information was inaccurate. A suggestion made by J.C. Cox in the 19th century that a voluntary militia was raised because of support for Prince amongst

the ordinary people of the town is not borne out by the small number of men who joined the Prince's army. It is possible, however, that the Prince was operating on false information fed to him by government agents. One of these, a Mr. Birch of London was discovered and imprisoned in Exeter House, but escaped through a window overlooking the Derwent and made his way downstream until rescued at Alvaston.

Having secured Swarkestone Bridge the Prince was well placed to continue south, but he turned back at Derby. This was probably because he had received advice of the advance of the 'Butcher' Duke of Cumberland and his army. However, the town was surprised by the retreat and had expected the rebels when they left to march towards Swarkestone instead of turning back towards Ashbourne. Perhaps the lack of success in recruiting in Derby also had some bearing on the Prince's action. Although he had taken Swarkestone Bridge he did not have enough men to hold it. In the 16th century, during the Lincolnshire Rebellion, the Earl of Shrewsbury had identified Swarkestone Bridge and Derby as the key points that he would need to hold to secure the south of the kingdom. He estimated that he would need at least 10,000 men to do this. The rebel army including camp followers only amounted to 7,000. Whatever the reason, the Prince took the decision not to continue south but to take his highlanders back to Scotland. At 7 a.m. on Friday, 30 November the pipers roused the rebels, and they left the town taking the road by which they had come. The Prince, riding a black horse, left at nine o'clock. He rode across the market place, down Sadlergate and away along the Ashbourne Road. By 11 o'clock the last rebel had left the town, and although no market was held that day life returned to normal.

Many of the rebels met their death on Culloden Moor. The Prince became a fugitive, fled across the Highlands to the Isle of Skye from whence he returned to France. The *Derby Mercury* joyfully reported the celebrations that followed the news of the victory at Culloden. The church bells were rung, and a large bonfire was constructed on which effigies of the Prince and the Pope were burnt. On 2 June 1746 the town sent a loyal address to the King celebrating the defeat of the rebels. It recorded that Culloden was a 'Victory never to be effaced from our memory'.[10]

46   Swarkestone Bridge across the River Trent, which Prince Charles's troops captured. This was the prince's gateway to the south and the conquest of London.

DERBY MERCURY.

From FRIDAY *April* 25. *to* FRIDAY *May* 2. 1746.   [Price *Two-Pence.*]

SATURDAY's POST.

From the London Gazette Extraordinary, *April* 23.

Whitehall, April 23.

This Day at Noon an Exprefs arrived from Edinburgh, with Letters dated the 19th Inftant, which brought the following Account.

HAT on Wednefday the 16th Inft. about Two o'Clock in the Afternoon, his Royal Highnefs the Duke of Cumberland came up with about 7000 of the Rebels on the Moor above Culloden near Invernefs, (*a Town of the County of Murray, in the North of Scotland,* 112 *Miles from Edinburgh.*) The Cannonading continued near a Quarter of an Hour; after which, the Right Wing of the Rebel Army, confifting of the Macdonalds and Frafers, advanced and attacked our Left; but after receiving two Fires, which did great Execution, they fled, with the reft of their Army, leaving 500 kill'd on the Field of Battle. They were purfued by the Horfe, Dragoons, and Argyllfhire Men; and it is computed full as many fell in the Flight. The French furrender'd themfelves Prifoners. Part of the Rebels fled towards Badenoch and Fort Auguftus; others thro' Invernefs to Rofsfhire. His Royal Highnefs the Duke enter'd Invernefs about Five that Night.

47 *(left)* News of Culloden in the *Derby Mercury.*

48 *(right)* Prince Charles as an old and disappointed man.

49 *(below)* *Lochaber No More,* a romantic Victorian view of Prince Charles leaving the shores of Great Britain forever which contrasts strongly with the relief felt by the population of the country at the time.

Chapter Seven

Turnpikes, Canals and the Enlightenment—
Derby in the Late 18th Century

◆

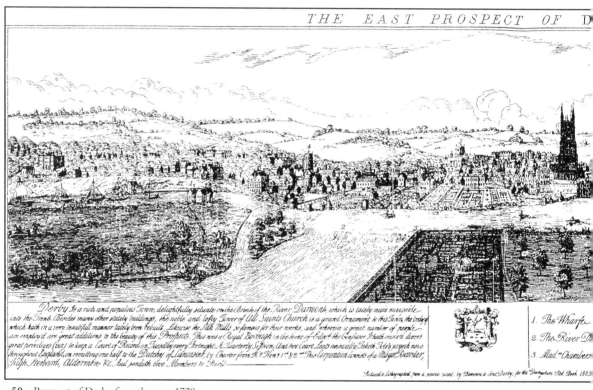

THE EAST PROSPECT OF D

Derby is a rich and populous Town, delightfully situate on the Brink of the River Derwent, which is lately made navigable into the Trent. Besides many other stately buildings, the noble and lofty Tower of All Saints Church is a grand Ornament to this Town, the body of which hath in a very beautifull manner lately been rebuilt. Likewise the Silk Mills so famous for their works, and wherein a great number of people are employ'd are great additions to the beauty of this Prospect. This was a Royal Borough in the time of Edwd the Confessor & hath men in divers great priviledges (viz) to keep a Court of Records on Tuesday every Fortnight, A Quarterly Session, And two Court Leets annually. Taketh Tole & payeth none throughout England, on remitting one half to the Dutchy of Lancaster, by Charter from K:9 Hen: 1482nd This Corporation consists of a Mayor, Recorder, High Steward, Aldermen &c. And sendeth two Members to Parlt

1. The Wharfe
2. The River D
3. Madm Chambers

Reduced & Lithographed from a scarce print by Bemrose & Sons Derby, for the Derbyshire Red Book 1863

50 Prospect of Derby from the east, 1728.

In the early 18th century most inland travel took place on the roads. Derby was connected to London by road, and carriers plied between the capital and the town, taking five days to complete a single journey. Roads across the country were in bad repair. In 1696 for example the quarter sessions records report that the road across Sinfin Moor was rendered impassable by sludge and mire.

Each parish was responsible for the repair of any stretch of highway that passed through it, but many parishes avoided doing repairs as they were

time consuming and expensive. However, at the end of the 17th century some parishes felt that they would be more inclined to repair the roads if they could charge those who used them. The Justices of the Peace in Hertfordshire took the initiative and in 1663 an Act of Parliament was passed which allowed the justices of Cambridgeshire, Hertfordshire and Huntingdonshire to levy tolls on road users. This was the first turnpike road, so called because a toll was collected at gates on the road, and a turnpike was a gate with moveable bars.

It did not take long for businessmen to realise that profits could be made from these roads, and for groups of entrepreneurs to form trusts to invest money in order to set up a turnpike. Turnpike trusts were formed by a private Act of Parliament which allowed the investors to improve the roads, set up barriers across them and to charge those who wished to go through. The improved roads meant faster travel and better communications.

The earliest road to be turnpiked in Derbyshire opened in 1725, between Buxton and Chapel en le

The new road surfaces cut journey times considerably, from three days by coach from Derby to London in 1764 to one day by the end of the 18th century. Fast coaches went from Derby across the country, and inter-change stops meant that the town was connected to all points of the kingdom. A multitude of carriers and at least six coaches a day travelled between Derby and Nottingham. Coaching inns grew up on the routes of the fast coaches, providing refreshment for the passengers and fresh horses for the coaches. Many of the large stable yards can

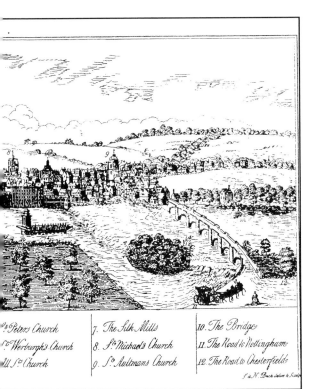

51   The *Bell Inn* in Sadlergate.

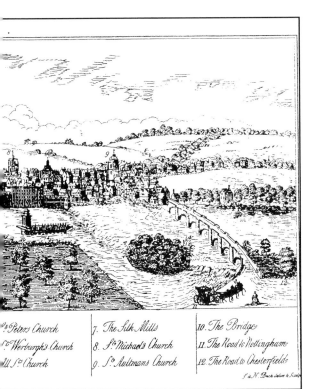

P. Peters Church   7. *The Silk Mills*   10. *The Bridge*
P. Werburgh's Church   8. *S.º Michael's Church*   11. *The Road to Nottingham*
All S.º Church   9. *S.º Auldman's Church*   12. *The Road to Chesterfield*

Frith. This was followed in 1738 by a road which crossed the Trent at Wilden Ferry and went on to Derby where it divided, with one branch going to Ashbourne through Brailsford, and the other through Quarndon, Hulland, Brassington and then northwards. The road between Derby and Burton on Trent was turnpiked in 1753, and that from Derby to Wirksworth in 1755. In 1759 the roads between Derby and Uttoxeter, and Derby and Nottingham were also turnpiked, and by 1791 eight turnpike roads converged on Derby.

still be seen in these old coaching inns, such as the *Bell* in Sadlergate, or the *George* in Irongate which was attached to the main postal office of the town.

Other evidences for turnpikes are the toll houses where the fee to use the road was collected by the gatekeeper who lived in the house with his family. Toll houses had polygonal projections with windows all the way round so that the gate keeper could see all the approaches to his gate. A board would have been placed on the outside of the house listing the tariffs that the traveller had to pay.

52 Toll house in Kedleston Road. Note that the toll road was on the garden side of the hedge.

A good example of a toll house can be seen on Kedleston Road. This faces away from the present road towards the line of Old Kedleston Road which still survives, marked by lines of trees through the University of Derby's grounds, and in the slip roads which run parallel to the new road. Another example of a toll house can be seen in Burton Road, and a further toll house stood at the corner of Mansfield Road in Little Chester. Seven gates stood between this gate and Mansfield, and the traveller was required to pay a toll at each.

Turnpikes were also marked by milestones which became compulsory after 1766. Examples of these can be seen on most roads leading out of Derby, and on the Uttoxeter Road where a post marks the boundary between the borough and the parish of Mickleover.

The turnpikes meant that road travel became fast and convenient for travellers, but road haulage was still very slow and expensive when it came to transporting heavy goods. Bulky goods such as coal and bricks had to be transported by water, which meant that many inland areas were inaccessible. On the continent canals had been developed to carry heavy goods, and were much admired by young English gentlemen doing the 'Grand Tour'. One of these was the Duke of Bridgewater who owned coal mines in south Lancashire. Increased competition cut off his market in Liverpool and in order to open up a new market in Manchester, the Duke built a canal which ran directly from his mines to the centre

of the city. The price of coal fell, but the Duke's profits rose. Other coal owners and manufacturers viewed this with interest, and soon formed companies in order to build their own canals. Canal mania had started.

After the opening of the Trent-Mersey and Grand Junction canals it looked as if Derby would be literally left in a backwater. Access to these important waterways which linked the ports of Liverpool and Hull was only possible from Derby through expensive road haulage to Shardlow. It was obvious to Derby's businessmen and manufacturers that a link was needed between Derby and the canal network.

On 12 September 1791 the *Derby Mercury* noted that application was to be made to obtain a private Act of Parliament for the making and maintaining of a navigable cut or canal from the Trent and Mersey canal through to Derby. The promoters of the scheme claimed that the new canal would be directed to the convenience of agriculture, the extension of commerce and the relief of the poor. In order to prove their commitment to the latter they promised that if the act was passed they would supply 5,000 tons of coal for the use of the poor.

The group proposing the new canal included important local landowners such as Sir Robert Wilmot of Osmaston, mill owners like William Evans

53 Road marker on the Kedleston toll road.

Derby and Swarkſtone intended Canals.

A
STATEMENT
OF THE

Advantage and Public Utility of theſe CANALS, compared with thoſe projected from DERBY to SHARDLOW and NOTTINGHAM.

THE Derby and Swarkſtone Scheme will open Communications with Collieries in different Places, and thereby prevent a Monopoly.

It will ſupply the Inhabitants of the Town and Neighbourhood of Derby with Coal, and bring Merchandize from the Weſt to that Town, cheaper than the Shardlow Canal, even if navigated on that Line free of Tonnage.

Beſides theſe Advantages, Lime and Merchandize from the Eaſt will be carried to Derby and its Vicinity, at conſiderably leſs Expence on theſe Canals than on that to Shardlow.

The Promoters of the Derby and Swarkſtone Canals have agreed to navigate 5000 Tons of Coal annually, Tonnage free, for the Benefit of the Poor of Derby.

The Saving to the Public by adopting the Derby and Swarkſtone Scheme inſtead of the Derby and Shardlow, will be upwards of £1500 a Year.

The Length of the ſeveral Lines of the Derby and Swarkſtone is Twenty-four Miles, and the Land Owners of Twenty-three Miles have aſſented thereto.

The Derby and Swarkſtone Scheme has the Sanction of the Corporation of Derby in Common Hall aſſembled, and was UNANIMOUSLY APPROVED OF AT A PUBLIC AND NUMEROUS Meeting of the Inhabitants of that Town and Neighbourhood, held at the County Hall in Derby the 8th of September laſt.

The Length of the Lines on the Derby and Shardlow is Fourteen Miles, and the Land Owners of not more than Four have given their Conſent.

The Derby and Shardlow Scheme has been projected and ſettled only in PRIVATE PARTIES, the Promoters having never ventured to call a Public Meeting for ſanctioning it.

The Promoters of the Derby and Swarkſtone Canals have propoſed to indemnify the Grand Trunk Company from every Loſs or Injury that can ariſe to them by this Undertaking.

54   Statement supporting the route of the Derby canal.

and William Strutt, corn merchants, bankers and coal merchants. The project quickly attracted shareholders, with shares changing hands at £20 each. Some shares were withheld from the stock market in order to be raffled off in a lottery.

Not everyone agreed with the scheme. There was a pamphlet war against the canal by those who objected to all such undertakings, and also by the projectors of a rival scheme which wanted to cut a canal from Shardlow to Nottingham.

The route the Derby canal was to take was to go from Swarkestone to Derby, with branches to Sandiacre to join the Erewash canal, and to Little Eaton. The Act to set this in motion received Royal Assent in May 1793. The Derby Canal Company met for the first time at the *Bell Inn* in Sadlergate on 1 July of that year.

Work on the canal started on 6 July 1793. The company appointed George Wootton as Super-intendent of Works at a salary of £150 a year, and a book keeper, William White, was hired with a salary of £105 a year. He was to keep a credit and debt account. Between them Wootton and White were to oversee day-to-day work on the canal, whilst the project's engineer Benjamin Outram was in overall charge. In all the project employed 600 workmen. By June 1794 the company could report to the shareholders that 14 miles of canal were cut, eight out of 46 bridges built, and three locks out of 17 were finished.

Navigating canals through the countryside was heavy and dangerous work. The canal company minute books show accidents to the workmen, and the amount of compensation paid to them. For example, the company minutes for 10 November 1794 order that 'five pounds be paid by the treasurer to Mr. White to be applied by him towards the expense of maintaining Antony Lowe a labourer upon the Canal whose leg was broken in an accident'. A further payment of £5 was made for Lowe's maintenance on 28 March 1795. The minutes also record compensation for damage to crops incurred as the 'navvies' worked.

Work was complicated because Sir Robert Wilmot insisted that the canal be sunk out of view of Osmaston Hall, and a bank had to be built to protect William Duesbury's china factory in Nottingham Road. This bank was breached in December 1799. On 9 December 1799 the company minutes note a request from Mr. Duesbury's china works for the urgent repair of the canal bank, and for compensation of £100 for china clay damaged in the flooding which occurred when the bank broke.

As the canal was being built toll houses went up as well. The toll collectors were to get £35 4s. a year and a house, but those appointed had to pay a surety of £200 in case they made off with the takings. The company minutes show that the canal toll house keepers were allowed to do other jobs as well. Joseph Cubley, for example, who was keeper on the town stretch of the canal, was given permission to continue his trade as a flax dresser, as well as collecting tolls.

The northern end of the canal at Little Eaton was to be linked to the Derbyshire coalfield by a horse-drawn railway. The first load of coal arrived from this railway on the wharf at Little Eaton on the morning of 11 May 1795, and was unloaded from a barge in Derby later the same afternoon. The whole canal system was completed by 30 June 1796.

The northern branch of the Derby canal was built for transporting coal, whilst corn, bricks and other materials were carried on the Sandiacre branch. Clay, tiles and cement were important commodities loaded on at Swarkestone. Good quality stone from the Little Eaton quarries was also carried on the canal. A passenger service ran from Swarkestone to the Friday market at Derby, charging a fare of 6d. return.

The company minutes of 12 September 1803 give an analysis of the tonnage of coal carried in the preceding six years.

Year	Other Coal	Derbyshire Coal	Total (in tons)
1797–8	17,041	11,530	28,571
1798–9	14,665	10,003	21,668
1799–1800	19,562	18,178	37,741
1800–1	No records kept		
1801–2	23,748	20,584	44,332
1802–3	22,603	27,771	50,374

The canal company's property in the centre of Derby was the prey of vandals and thieves. In 1828 the company had to hire a watchman to guard the Cockpit Hill wharf. Close to this the canal towpath crossed the Derwent on a wooden bridge

55   Siddall's canal lock in 1874.

which was demolished in 1959. Damage also occurred on the company's property at Little Eaton. In September 1798 a handbill was published offering a five-guinea reward for information about vandals who were strewing nails on the railway track.

Opposition and vandalism as well as the heavy capital investment needed to build the canal meant that the early years of the canal were unprofitable for the shareholders. No dividends were paid between 1797 and 1801, but in 1802 a two and a half per cent dividend was paid. This rose to four per cent in 1806, but extensive repairs were needed to the banks and locks in the first decade of the 19th century which cut back dividends again. Although by 1817 the shareholders were receiving dividends of six and a half per cent, nobody made a fortune from the Derby canal.[1]

Until the coming of the railway the canal was the chief carrier of heavy goods in the area, but the railways were a fierce rival to the canal. In 1840 the canal company was involved in a price cutting war to win back trade lost to the railways. The toll for coal was reduced from 1s. 5d. a ton to 8d. a ton. Eventually the canal company offered to sell the canal to the railway companies but failed. The canal

continued to carry coal throughout the 19th and early 20th centuries. In 1929, 11,200 tons of goods were carried, but the amount fell rapidly after this date. In 1931 the Little Eaton end of the canal was closed, and the demolition started of some of the canal buildings. In 1958 the flow of water to the Swarkestone branch was stopped. Some effort was made to reverse the decay in the early 1960s, but in 1964 a warrant was issued to permit the abandonment of the canal. The whole enterprise was wound up in 1974. Today, however, efforts are being made to revive the canal as a leisure facility.

The 18th century saw the development of new and exciting ideas based on scientific theory and experimentation. Men began to question the whole nature of the universe. They wanted to know why it was constructed as it was, how things worked and to classify and catalogue the natural world. This climate of inquiry was led by men from the professions and industry who took a keen interest in science and technology. One such man was Erasmus Darwin, the youngest son of William Darwin of Elston in Nottinghamshire. Born in 1731, after attending Chesterfield School and St John's College, Cambridge, Darwin went to Edinburgh to study medicine. In 1757, after a disastrous start to his medical career in Nottingham, he moved to Lichfield where he became a popular physician.

Darwin was a free thinker with a lively mind. Together with other like-minded men such as James Watt, Benjamin Franklin and Josiah Wedgwood he formed a society which met once a month in one of the members' houses to discuss philosophical and scientific matters. The society was known as the Lunar Society, and from its base in Birmingham it was to become one of the leading laboratories for scientific experiments in the country.

In 1781 Darwin, whose first wife Mary had died, was remarried to the widow of Colonel Chandos Pole, and for three years lived with his new wife in Radbourne Hall. Later they moved to Full Street in Derby, and from there to Breadsall Priory. In 1783 Darwin, with nine other gentlemen, founded the Philosophical Society of Derby for the purpose of discussing intellectual arguments and undertaking scientific experiments. By 1829 the Philosophical Society had its own premises in St

57   A clock made by John Whitehurst and Co.—now in the Industrial Museum, Derby.

Helen's Street, a membership of 46, a library, its own mathematical and philosophical apparatus and a collection of fossils and other specimens.

The Philosophical Society built on a tradition of intellectual inquiry already present amongst the town's tradesmen, such as Benjamin Parker, a stocking-maker of Bridge Street who published a series of philosophical meditations, and Robert Bage, a paper mill owner and old friend of William Hutton who worked on the definition of a system of knowledge. Outside the town Abraham Bennet of Matlock experimented with electricity which Darwin helped to publicise in his books. Darwin believed that experimentation was the key to knowledge, as shown in the first address he gave to the Philosophical Society. He put heavy emphasis on experimentation, as he stated his belief that 'A fool is a man who has never tried an experiment in his life'.[2]

Another noted scientist who had connections with Derby was John Whitehurst, the horologist, geologist and mathematician who set up business in Derby in 1736. His interest in minerals led him to explore the geological foundations of the earth and in 1778 he published one of the first treatises on geology and the origins of the earth called *An Inquiry into the Original State and Formation of the Earth.*

One man who was much influenced by the experiments carried out by the Derby Philosophical Society was Joseph Wright the artist. Wright was born in 1734 at 23 Irongate, the youngest son of

PHYTOLOGIA;

OR THE

PHILOSOPHY

OF

AGRICULTURE

AND

GARDENING.

WITH THE THEORY OF DRAINING MORASSES,

AND WITH AN

IMPROVED CONSTRUCTION OF THE DRILL PLOUGH.

By ERASMUS DARWIN, M.D. F.R.S.

AUTHOR OF ZOONOMIA, AND OF THE BOTANIC GARDEN.

Suadent hæc CREATORIS leges a fimplicibus ad compofita.   LIN. ORD. NAT.

LONDON:

PRINTED FOR J. JOHNSON, ST. PAUL'S CHURCH-YARD;

BY T. BENSLEY, BOLT COURT, FLEET STREET.

1800.

56   Title page of a work by Erasmus Darwin which shows the wide range of his interests.

John Wright an attorney. He was educated at Derby grammar school where his talent for drawing was evident from an early age. In 1751 he was placed with Thomas Hudson of London to learn the trade of portrait painting. When he returned to Derby after a spell with Hudson he was able to pick up local commissions for his work. One of the first of these was a painting of the Derby Hunt, which showed a collection of local worthies in hunting dress with their fine horses. It was a good advertisement for Wright's work and he soon produced a remarkable series of portraits of Derbyshire characters. These not only included the gentry set in their estates, but industrialists such as Sir Richard Arkwright, shown in the full bloom of his success, testing his water frame spinning machine. Wright also painted Jedediah Strutt, John White-hurst the clockmaker, Erasmus Darwin and other members of the Lunar Society.

It was through his friendship with Darwin that Wright gained access to the experiments shown so vividly in his paintings, *A Philosopher giving a Lecture*

59   William Hutton at the age of eighty.

on the Orrery and *The Experiment on a Bird in an Air Pump*, which can be seen with other notable works by Wright in the city museum.

Wright was fascinated by light. He painted pictures which had strong effects of light and shade, and specialised in candlelight illuminating figures with the rest of the picture in shadow. He was also one of the first artists to record scenes of the Industrial Revolution, showing how the mills, foundries and factories turned night into day with lights burning all night for the night shift, and furnaces lighting the sky with red flames. Wright spent most of his professional life in Derby. He died at his house in Queen Street in 1797.

Wright would have been able to observe the effect of forges and furnaces at first hand in Derby. There were slitting and rolling mills preparing iron by the Derwent and on the Morledge, the Britannia Foundry in Duke Street, and the Faulkner forge in Chester Road, where fine wrought iron was produced.

Another Derby worthy of the 18th century whose life is a rags-to-riches story was William Hutton, the antiquarian. Born in Full Street in 1723, he was given a brief education before being put into

58   Joseph Wright.

The Arms of Derby Town.

DERBYSHIRE.

This County, which lies in the Middle of England, borders on the North upon Yorkshire, on the East upon Nottinghamshire, on the South upon Leicestershire & Warwickshire, and on the West upon Staffordshire and Cheshire. Its principal River is the Derwent, which crosses it from North-West to South-East: Besides which it has the Dove, in great Part its Western Boundary, the Erwash, and a little of the Trent and the Mersey.

The Eastern Parts of Derbyshire are pleasant & fertile, particularly in Barley: Nor is the Peak, or Western Part, destitute of Commodities among its Wonders. It has, however, a sharper, more various, and consequently less wholesom Air than the more level Country. Produce of y whole, besides Grain and Grass, is Lead, Antimony, Marble, Alabaster, a Coarse sort of Chrystal, Iron, Pit-Coal, and Grindstones.

Only four Members are sent hence to Parliament, two for the County, and two for the Capital Derby.

60 Elegant Derby. A page from an anonymous 18th-century description of the county.

a seven-year apprenticeship in the Silk Mill at the age of seven. When he had completed this in 1738 he started on another seven-year term with his uncle George Hutton, a silk stockinger of Nottingham. In 1745 he became a journeyman stockinger, but he had been teaching himself bookbinding and left the hosiery business to open a small book shop in Southwell. He moved to Birmingham in 1750, and made his living as a bookseller. He also started to collect the historical information which would form the nucleus of his books. By 1759 his fortune was such that he opened a paper mill in Handsworth. His history of Derby was published in 1791. That same year rioters sacked his house in Birmingham and, to prevent it being burnt to the ground, he is said to have bought the mob off with 329 gallons of ale. He moved to Bristol in 1792 and died in 1815.

Although Derby was becoming more industrialised in the 18th century, it was still very much a market town rather than an industrial centre. The gentry from the county flocked into the town to attend the races on Sinfin Moor, the opening of the Assizes and entertainments held in the Assembly rooms.

The gentry who attended the balls and races either leased or owned some of the fine 18th-century houses that can be seen in the centre of town. The most handsome examples are St Helen's House in King Street and Pickford's House in Friargate.

St Helen's House was built for the Gisburne family by Joseph Pickford. Joseph Pickford was born in 1734. He was the son of a stone mason from Warwick. In 1748 he was apprenticed to his uncle, another stone mason, and worked with him on the Horse Guards in Whitehall, and stately homes such as Holkham Hall in Norfolk. Pickford first appeared in Derbyshire in 1759 when he was one of the masons working on Foremark Hall. When he married Mary Wilkins of Longford in 1762 he was described as living in St Peter's parish, Derby. By this time he was building houses of his own design. His solid and harmonious designs attracted a number of noble patrons. He was employed in remodelling Tissington for the Fitz-Herberts, and also built houses for the Meynell and Beresford families. His most notable patron was the Duke of Devonshire. He worked at Edensor and Chatsworth for the Duke. In Derby he remodelled Bess of Hardwick's almshouses in Full Street for the Duke in 1777. Pickford created a classically-inspired complex of single-storied cottages set around a courtyard, decorated with the Cavendish coat of arms, and described in 1782 as being inconvenient for the aged inhabitants.

61   St Helen's House.

Pickford was to be ridiculed about the Duke's patronage in an anonymous pamphlet in which he was described as a 'servile sycophant'. The occasion was Pickford's election to be an honorary burgess in 1776, just prior to an election in which Pickford could then vote for the Duke's party.

Pickford's most notable achievements in Derby were the Friargate development and St Helen's House. St Helen's House is a fine Palladian-style house which relies on balance for effect. The sides and rear of the house are built of brick, but the front is made of finely worked stone known as ashlar, which has a smooth almost silky finish. The mortar on the ground floor at the front of the house is recessed so that the stones stand out in relief. This is known as rustication, and it gives the house an appearance of great strength and solidity. On the corners of the roof are delicately wrought stone urns.

Pickford's House was built in 1770. It is a three-storied house of red brick with stone picking out the essential features. It has a fine central doorway with steps leading up to the entrance which is guarded by elegant pillars. Pickford is also known to have built 44 and 45 Friargate; no. 44 was built for John Ward, a silk throwster and 45 for his partner Daniel Lowe, a hosier.

Good quality 18th-century houses are to be found throughout Derby. They can be identified by their characteristic rectangular sash windows with the panes divided by glazing bars into three smaller panes across and four down. The architectural decoration of these houses is concentrated on the front entrance which is often approached by stone steps leading to a canopied porch and a front door graced by a traceried fan-light. Examples of these houses can be seen on both sides of Friargate. These usually have three storeys and were built of brick with details picked out in stone, and are probably the work of Joseph Pickford.

Pickford died in 1782 and was buried in St Werburgh's Church. Although there is no memorial to him in the church, the lasting quality of his houses make a fitting monument to his achievements.

Pickford was one of the many members of Derby's élite who were involved in the failure of Heaths' Bank in 1779, as the money he had used to buy plots in Friargate had been borrowed from the Heaths. Heath's bank had premises in Lock Up Yard in the Cornmarket which Pickford had designed.

62   Pickford's House in Friargate.

The Heaths, John and Christopher, were using depositors' money from their bank to buy up mortgages, foreclose and sell the properties for a profit. Unfortunately their greed overtook their caution and they went bankrupt, exposing their shady dealings and implicating many of Derby's leading citizens including Thomas Rivett MP, William Duesbury of the china works, Thomas Evans MP, Hugh Bateman, Francis Mundy of Markeaton Hall and Edward Mundy of Shipley Hall.

The Heaths had numerous business interests. John was described as a maltster, and also had a third share in the Cockpit potworks with Thomas Rivett and William Duesbury, as well as being a partner in Duesbury's china works in Nottingham Road. Both brothers were aldermen and served terms as mayors, John in 1759-60 and Christopher in 1774.

The full extent of their shady dealings is difficult to disentangle. The bank lent money at four to five per cent interest either as a bonded loan, or with property put up as collateral. One convoluted transaction shows how the Heath's under-hand if not actually illegal business methods worked. In 1750 Ambrose Ratten an innholder took out a 500-year lease on a property in Stanley which belonged to John Fletcher of Stainsby. The price of the lease was

63 18th-century house in Full Street, reputed to be the house of John Heath the defaulting banker.

£500 on which Ratten had to pay Fletcher four per cent interest. By 1753 no interest had been paid so the premises were forfeit. In April 1753 John Heath agreed to pay the £500 from Ratten to Fletcher as part of a £1,000 loan he was making to Fletcher, providing that the premises and Ratten's mortgage were assigned to the bank. In effect Heath had manoeuvred Fletcher into accepting as a loan the £500 which was rightfully his from Ratten, and at the same time had acquired rights in the property.

Fletcher was to repay the loan at two per cent interest by 4 October 1753, and gave Heath a bond for £2,000 as security. In 1775 loan interest and bond were still unpaid, but Heath had acquired more of Fletcher's property as security. When the bank went bankrupt members of the Fletcher family were required by the court to repay the money that John Fletcher had borrowed so that the bank could satisfy its creditors. These included their clerks Joseph Hill and Elbro Woodcock, and their servants who sued them for wages worth £257 0s. 2d. Thomas Evans and Walter Mather, who acted as the Heaths' receivers, were still trying to sell the bank's property and sort out its finances in 1785.[3]

64 The *Wardwick Tavern* showing the carriage entry and pediment hiding the roof.

Heath's bank was not the only bank to fail in Derby. On 21 August 1815 Bellairs Bank was declared bankrupt by Messrs Down, Thornton & Co, the London bank that they drew on which called in bills worth £20. This was part of a general economic panic following the end of the Napoleonic wars when the economic recession and inflation led to a withdrawal of savings from banks and the calling in of old debts. Small banks all over the country crashed in 1815-16.[4]

Another example of an 18th-century building is the *Wardwick Tavern*, built in the 1740s, this time without the exuberant decoration of some of the Friargate houses, but possessing the characteristic rectangular windows. The *Friary Hotel* in Friargate and the Friargate House School are other fine examples of 18th-century houses in Derby.

It is always a good idea to look above the modern frontages on the ground floor of buildings in the centre of Derby as architectural details are likely to survive on the first floor. A good example of this is the 17th-century Jacobean House in the Wardwick. This is a four-storey red brick house with stone dressings and mullioned windows. Also from the 17th century is the *Seven Stars* inn in King Street which is constructed of brick now painted white with black brick mouldings, giving the false impression of half-timbering.

Before the use of brick most of the buildings in the town would have been built of timber framing with panels of wattle and daub. No. 22 Irongate is a timber-framed building which dates from about 1540. Close to this building is the site of the *Talbot Inn*, which was an inn from the medieval period onwards. One of the best preserved timber-framed buildings in the town is the *Old Dolphin* public house, which has been an inn since 1580.

All Saints' Church, which was in poor repair at the beginning of the 18th century, was remodelled by its incumbent Dr. Hutchinson in 1723. However,

65   *Ye Olde Dolphin* public house.

the parishioners who were attached to their old church objected to the new plans, and the corporation would not give permission for the rebuilding. Dr. Hutchinson took matters into his own hands and during the night of 18 February 1723 had the interior of the church demolished and the roof removed so that there was no option but to rebuild. The corporation which had responsibility for the upkeep of the chancel refused to give any funds for its rebuilding so that Hutchinson was forced to raise the money himself through an appeal. The subscribers who gave to the work included Sir Robert Walpole and Isaac Newton.

66   Interior of All Saints' as remodelled in the 18th century by Dr. Hutchinson and showing Bakewell's screen.

Hutchinson was in continuous dispute with the corporation and his parishioners. This resulted in an unseemly brawl in the church between the mayor and his mace bearers, and church officials.

Despite its unpopularity at the time, Hutchinson gave the town a building of the finest quality 18th-century architecture. It was designed by James Gibb in a classical style. The interior which is now painted white and lilac is light and spacious, and includes a fine wrought-iron chancel screen made by Robert Bakewell in 1752 when it cost £200. As well as the Cavendish vault there are 18th- and early 19th-century monuments which continue the classical theme, and enrich the harmony of the building. All Saints' with its impressive Perpendicular tower is a landmark of which the town can be justifiably proud.

Although 18th-century Derby was at the forefront of the Industrial Revolution, the town was still closely connected with the land. Friargate and Ashbourne Road were surrounded by open land, Burton Road and Old Uttoxeter Roads ran through fields, and Litchurch, Allestree, Mickleover, Sinfin and Chaddesden were still isolated hamlets. However, the need for increased food production

as the population of the town grew, led to the enclosure of common land and the old open fields.

In 1768 part of the town's common grazing land at Nuns Green was enclosed and sold. The remaining 48 acres were boggy waste land crossed by the Markeaton Brook, and it was claimed that it was no longer used for grazing but instead provided a haunt for robbers and footpads, and a dangerous place to cross after dark.

By the end of the 18th century it was felt that Derby in general was a dangerous and un-wholesome place to be after dark. The streets were unlit, and were made doubly perilous because they were not paved. The pedestrians had to pick their way through deep mud, puddles and cess pits so that it was difficult to arrive at a destination dry shod and clean. Other towns and cities were taking out private Acts of Parliament to enable them to pave and light their streets. Derby wished to follow suit, but did not wish to burden its rate-payers with extra rates and taxes to pay for it. In order to prevent this it was proposed by the burgesses, led by William Strutt, that the remaining unenclosed land at Nuns Green should be sold for building, and the proceeds spent on improving the town. On 23 November 1789 a general public meeting was held in order to appoint a committee to prepare a plan for paving and lighting the streets. Taking the improvement of Liverpool as a model, the committee started to estimate the cost of improving Derby.

Prior to the suggestion that the sale of Nuns Green could finance the improvement it had seemed to the corporation that few people used the green. Once it was suggested that this land would be sold, a vociferous opposition appeared which saw that with the loss of this land would go the loss of important rights of access, and a general infringement of personal freedom. A vigorous debate

Paving and Lighting,

A NEW SONG.

To the Tune of Chivy Chaſe.

GOD proſper long fair DERBY Town,
  And may it ſtill be free ;
From helliſh plots of every kind,
  Againſt its liberty,

A juncto formed of wicked men,
  Though rich its true they be ;
They'd rob the poor of Common-right,
  That they may go ſhot free.

The Preſbyterians Jeſuit like,
  The eſtabliſhed Church took in ;
To do the drudgery of their work,
  And trudged through thick and thin.

Poor ſilly men to be miſled,
  By that deceitful race ;   (back,
That would cut your throat behind your
  But ſmile before your face.

From the Town-hall they iſſue forth,
  With Eunuch at their head ;
Lazarus the Banker followed him,
  You'd have thought they wanted bread.

Next one from beggar's blood that ſprung,
  To opulence grown is he ;
And ſtruts along with iron rod,
  And ſwears you ſhan't be free:

A tawny Smith was of the gang,
  And others as well as he ;
They've neither houſe nor land in town,
  Yet want your property:

A brazen face with empty ſcull,
  In Dibden's Tour well known ;
That cares not what he does or ſays,
  So that the poor's o'erthrown.

Sly Foxes too with ſilly hopes,
  Expect to have their ſhare ;

Of all the Common-right you have,
  Their pockets for to ſpare.

Lo ! deep in thought as Tragic Muſe,
  With dagger to ſtab behind ;
Lo ! another as bad as he,
  And much of the ſame kind.

The Scribbling kind with parchment roll,
  For you to ſign away,
The Right you have upon Nun's-Green,
  Their charges to defray.

There are many others of the gang,
  As bad as bad can be ;
That lie, fawn, and threat, and uſe deceit,
  To get your property.

Old Shot-bag he has chang'd about,
  That his Mills may go ſhot-free ;
Some others too have done the ſame,
  Such worthleſs men there be.

But all's a blank that they have done,
  If you but true will be ;
To the firſt promiſe that was made,
  The friends to liberty.

Now Mundy's join'd with **Parker** Coke,
  And others of renown ;
Thoſe tyrants for to circumvent,
  To ſave this goodly town.

Thoſe veterans that have ſtood the brunt,
  Of many a well fought day ;
Will always cheer you in the front,
  And ſhew you the right way.

For to be free as Brittons ought,
  And have a right to be ;
In ſpite of theſe tyrannic fools,
  That want your liberty.

67 'Paving and Lighting'. One of the many ballads produced for and against the sale of Nuns Green.

took place between those for and against the sale, which was carried out in ballads, handbills, pamphlets and the press.

On 5 January 1791 a pamphlet signed by Dr. Erasmus Darwin was published which pointed out the advantage to the health of the citizens which would follow the cleansing and paving of the town's streets. Darwin wrote that such an act would 'contribute to the pleasure of the inhabitants and the dispatch of business'.

Darwin's views were echoed by a 'Lady' in a pamphlet called *An Address to the Ladies of Derby by one of their own sex*, which shows some very modern ideas. The anonymous author says that paving and lighting would give greater freedom for ladies who were confined indoors by bad streets, mud and the dark. She continues by describing her sister's return from a shopping expedition to buy a hat in town: 'My sister Sophia return'd from the Milliners this morning Splash'd up above her knees, the fringe of her petticoat stiff with dirt, and her fine auburn hair glued together like the quills of porcupine!'. When their brother suggested that she should have stayed at home, the author was so incensed she threw a cup of tea over him saying, 'What have we to do with Nuns in these days. Besides, brother, it belongs to us all, as well as to you; women have rights as well as men'. She exhorts the women of Derby to support the sale of the green and to encourage their husbands, sons and lovers to do likewise.

Those against the sale invoked ancient rights granted to them by John of Gaunt, and warned that the sale would destroy the town. One pamphlet by *Veritas* likened the sale to the French Revolution which raised the standard of freedom, whereas in Derby Whiggism, by stopping the sale, was suppressing liberty and creating tyranny.

Songs and ballads for and against the sale were published. Often those in opposition to the sale were referred to in the ballads as animals, such as the donkeys in *The Quadrupeds, or Four Footed Petitions against the Sale of Nuns Green*. This was described by its author as a *Terrestrial Poem by a Celestial Poet*:

Two Jack-Asses (the Father and his Son)
Who after work, on Nun's Green us'd to run
Exactly like two Bards; – the other day
Stood in a muse; – and then began to bray
With human voice; For Balaam's breed were they

Quoth Old Ned, to his lad; – I have been told
Nuns Green, my little dear, is to be sold
To pave, and light, Old Derbys fulsome town
And save the Poor from laying money down.
Now is it fair, that you and I shall be
Deprived of our just Rights, and Property?
It is an insult to the Jack-Ass kind
Who have possessed the green since time out of
   mind ...

An ironic pamphlet in favour of the scheme was in the form of a dialogue between Jerry Snip the tailor and Crispin Snob the Cobbler. It portrays the anti-sale lobby as alcoholics who did not want their activities seen:

If a Gentleman goes out at night hereafter to get soberly drunk in good company at the alehouse, everybody will see, by the Light of the Lamp, how one staggers about—Besides, if one should stay a little late, our wives, who are now afraid of the dark and the dirt, will come to fetch us home at midnight—and my wife is the very devil.

The pamphlet goes on to point out that paved streets will cut down on shoe repairs and so harm the trade of the cobbler; pasture for animals and healthy exercise such as skittles will be lost, whilst the draining of the marshy land would create flooding and the view from the gentlemen's houses in Friargate would be spoilt. The pamphlet ends by stating outright its real intention—to expose the stupidity of those opposing the sale: '... and it shall be to our glory, hereafter to have it published to the World, that Obstinacy, Selfishness, and Folly, have made Derby the dirtiest town in England'.

Both sides had extensive support in town. The opposition led by Daniel Parker Cole produced a large petition against the scheme. This stated that the petitioners were against the sale of the green because it was the common and equal property of all the inhabitants of Derby. When it was sent to Parliament, the document included a list of those who preferred to stay neutral.

On 29 March 1791 an unsuccessful attempt was made to get the two sides to agree to a compromise, and those who wanted improvement and the sale of the green pressed on regardless. The private Act enabling the corporation to sell the green went through Parliament in 1792. It allowed the corporation to pave the streets and light them by oil lamps. The act set up an Improvement Commission to manage the scheme and administer the money

A Birch Rod for the PRESBYTARIANS.

A NEW SONG.

TUNE of CHEVY CHACE.

GOOD neighbours all, both great and small,
   Of high and low degree ;
Let's straight unite, ourselves to fight,
   Against this presbytree.

If you'll but trace this hellish race,
   Thro' every stage of life ;
Where e'er they be you'll plainly see,
   Nought but discord and strife.

If you'll history read your hearts will bleed,
   To hear of their transactions ;
For king and church have suffered much,
   By their damn hellish factions.

Must we be opprest by this vile nest,
   Who strives us to enslave ;
Such is their spleen to sell Nun's Green,
   The town to light and pave.

They do not care who the burden bear,
   Such is their tyranny ;
To enforce the tax on others backs,
   Whilst they themselves go free.

I wish all such Aldermen and folks like them,
   Was forc'd to change their situation ;
And that Greenland hulks for their vile bulks,
   Might for ever be their station.

Proud oppulence with impudence,
   As he struts along the streets ;
Swears by his God with his iron rod,
   He'll beat down all he meets.

There's shuffling Charles both grins and snarles,
   And where he can he'll bite ;
For this last mishap he'll surely snap,
   Except he's muffeld tight.

There's Jemmy Twichit did both scrub and fidge it,
   His head he roll'd about ;
He stampt and swore he'd come there no more,
   When he found the bill thrown out.

They blam'd old George that did not discharge,
   His duty as he ought ;
And his addle pate that cou'd not relate,
   What kind of a bill he'd brought.

The wigs got a fall, I wish they ne'er may rise,
   But henceforth for the future, may learn to be more
      wise ;
And ne'er perfume to sit in chairs, nor honored be with
      Town affairs,
   But stay at home and say their prayers, & not over
      us tyrannize.

Pray God above from this earth remove,
   This vile deceitful crew,
And send them hence for their offence,
   Where they may receive their due.

God bless Mundy and Cooke, on them we look,
   As two from heaven sent ;
To set us free from tyranny,
   And serve in Parliament.

❖ ❖ ❖ ❖

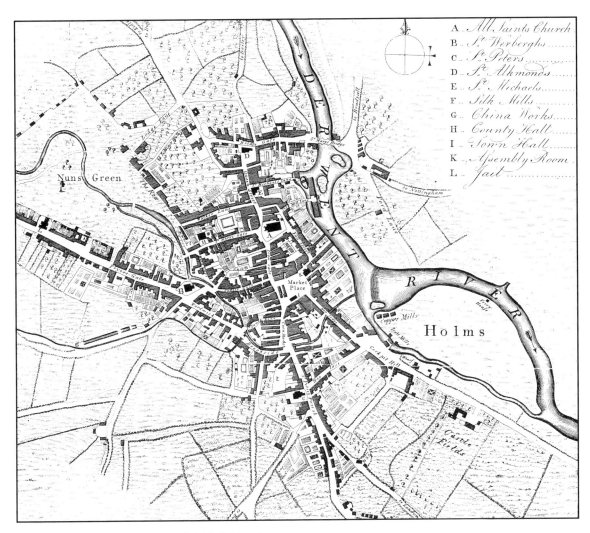

A... All Saints Church
B... St. Werberghs
C... St. Peters
D... St. Alkmonds
E... St. Michaels
F... Silk Mills
G... China Works
H... County Hall
I... Town Hall
K... Asembly Room
L... Gail

68 *(left)* 'Birch Rod for Presbyterians'. This ballad introduces a political theme to the debate on Nuns Green.

69 *(above)* Monypenny's 1791 map of Derby.

gained from the sale of the green. This became an important local government body which rivalled the power of the corporation.

Soon after the Act was passed and Nuns Green was sold to building speculators, the opposition accused the Improvement Commissioners of embezzling the money. It was claimed that the money from the sale was both being spent on improving the streets, and on 'prosecuting widows and orphans and in extending the suffrage through false means'.[5]

Despite the objections the town was vastly improved by the paving and lighting. But the sale of Nuns Green and the buildings erected on the site helped to divide the town further from the countryside, and very soon those working in manufacturing industries and retailing were to outnumber those living in the town who were involved in agriculture. The sale of Nuns Green, therefore, marks a break in the town's relationship with its surroundings and the start of modern Derby.

Chapter Eight

Early 19th-Century Derby

In 1829 Samuel Glover described Derby as 'rapidly increasing in population and improvement. The principle streets have recently been improved upon McAdam's plan and the footpaths are paved with stones or bricks. The houses are mostly built with red bricks which are made in the vicinity of the town.'[1]

The early 19th-century town had a good water supply coming either from wells in Becket Street, Friars Walk or Babington Lane, or a conduit in Bradshaw Street where the water gushed from the mouth of a stone lion. But those who could afford it had water piped into their houses from an ingenious method devised by the Water Company of pumping water from the River Derwent. It was then fed by gravity under the pavements along further wooden pipes to those consumers who paid the water company for the privilege. The water company had no purification plant, and the Derwent at this time was heavily polluted by factory and household waste, so the water coming from the taps into the gentry's houses was of doubtful quality. The

70   St John the Evangelist's Church.

water company was divided between three shareholders. Walter Evans of the cotton manufacturing family, a Mrs. Chambers and Joseph Strutt who represented the Improvement Commissioners. The company was a profit making concern, paying its shareholders regular dividends. A gas company was set up in 1826. It built two gasometers, but the gas it supplied was too expensive for domestic users to buy. The refusal of the customers to pay its high prices induced the Gas Company to cut its losses and lower its prices to persuade more householders to light their homes by gas.

The population of the borough was given as 13,145 in 1801. This rose to 15,719 in 1811, 21,459 in 1821 and 27,190 in 1831. The census return for that year shows that there were 5,129 houses in the town, occupied by 5,670 families, which suggests that there were some houses with more than one family living in them.

The increase in population meant that there were not enough parishes to serve everyone who either wanted to or should go to church, and it was felt that the morals of the working class would suffer accordingly. In order to circumvent this, new parishes were formed and new churches built. The earliest of these was St John the Evangelist in Mill Street. Its construction was the result of a meeting called to discuss the re-drawing of the large parish of St Werburgh. St John's was to be a free civic church with no pew rents. This upset the non-conformists in the town who thought that free seats would tempt their congregations away. Despite these objections the new church was consecrated on August 1828.

This was followed in 1836 by the gothic style Holy Trinity Church on the Castlefields estate in London Road. At first this church was dedicated to St George and, as befitted its dedication to the national saint, the interior was painted in red, white and blue. It was reputed to be a low church establishment with the Ten Commandments painted on the east end of the church. It also possessed an unusual glass and stone font. Another new church was Christ Church, built on the west side of Normanton Road in 1838. These new churches are evidence that the town was expanding rapidly away from the centre as new suburbs developed.

The Roman Catholic community in the town was also growing. In the early 19th century this was swollen by an influx of Irish immigrants seeking

71 *(top)* Late 19th-century drawing of the Roman Catholic chapel.

72 *(bottom)* St Mary's Roman Catholic Church, designed by Augustus Pugin and opened in 1839.

work in the mills. It soon outgrew the small chapel erected in 1813 and, with the aid of the Earl of Shrewsbury, a new church was planned. The up and coming young architect Augustus Pugin was hired to design the church, and the Roman Catholic Church of St Mary, which is a masterpiece of Victorian gothic, opened in 1839.

Other churches and chapels in the early 19th-century town included Baptist chapels in Brook and

73 *(top)* Late 19th-century drawing of the King Street Methodist chapel.

74 *(bottom)* Early 19th-century drawing of the Sweden-borgian New Jerusalem Chapel in London Road.

Agard Streets, a Methodist chapel in King Street, and two Swedenborgian chapels. The Sweden-borgians were a sect founded in Sweden by Count Emmanuel von Swedenborg. Their main belief was in the resurrection of the spirit rather than the body. It is rare for a provincial town to have one Swedenborgian congregation in it, but Derby had two. The initial connection between Derby and the Swedenborgians was the Madeley family, who were silk throwsters with two large mills in Cavendish Street. By 1818 the congregation was large enough to warrant the building of the New Jerusalem Chapel on London Road, and for another group led by James Robinson who was a draper to open another chapel. The two congregations amalgamated in 1836.

Although by 1831 most of the working population were employed in retailing or industry there were still some involved in agriculture. One hundred and fifty men in the town worked as agricultural labourers. Most of these lived in St Peter's parish. The town's connection with the countryside was also maintained by the corporation as it still had grazing rights on the Siddalls and Old Meadows. In 1831 the grazing rights and the hay from the meadows were leased to Messrs. Cox. The corporation could also graze animals on the Holmes, Chequer Close, Cowsley Fields and the New Pastures. Open spaces in the town were used by gentlemen and their grooms to exercise their horses. Livestock was sold at the cattle market on Cockpit Hill, and slaughtered in The Butchery on the west side of the market place.

Professional men such as lawyers and doctors were plentiful in the town. Skilled mechanics worked in industries such as John Smith's clock-making works. In St Helen's and King Streets there were spar and marble works where Blue John from the Peak and Chellaston marble was sawn and polished to be turned into chimney pieces and ornaments. The Blue John works became an essential place for tourists to Derby to visit, one of whom was Dr. Samuel Johnson.

The 180-ft. shot tower erected in 1809 on the Morledge also impressed visitors. Lead was melted at the top of the tower, poured into a pan perforated with holes, from whence it fell into a cistern at the bottom of the tower to be cooled in water. Other engineering works in early 19th-century Derby included Fox and Sons' engine and lathe factory, and Harrison's engine boiler house. There were also colour mills and a saw mill on the Derwent, and a lace factory in Castle Street. There were at least 10 printing firms in the town. One of the oldest of these was that of Henry Mosley which opened in 1815. William Bemrose's printing shop appeared at the same time. The printers in the town prospered greatly and, as well as doing jobbing printing, were also publishers in their own right. Bemrose produced novels, directories and poll books, as well as other publications.

The success of the printing firms was due partly to an increase in literacy and a determined campaign by reformers to teach children to read. In Derby the campaign saw the opening of a number of new schools. In 1812 a National School for Poor

75 *(right)* 1806 map of Derby engraved by J. Roper from a drawing by G. Cole.

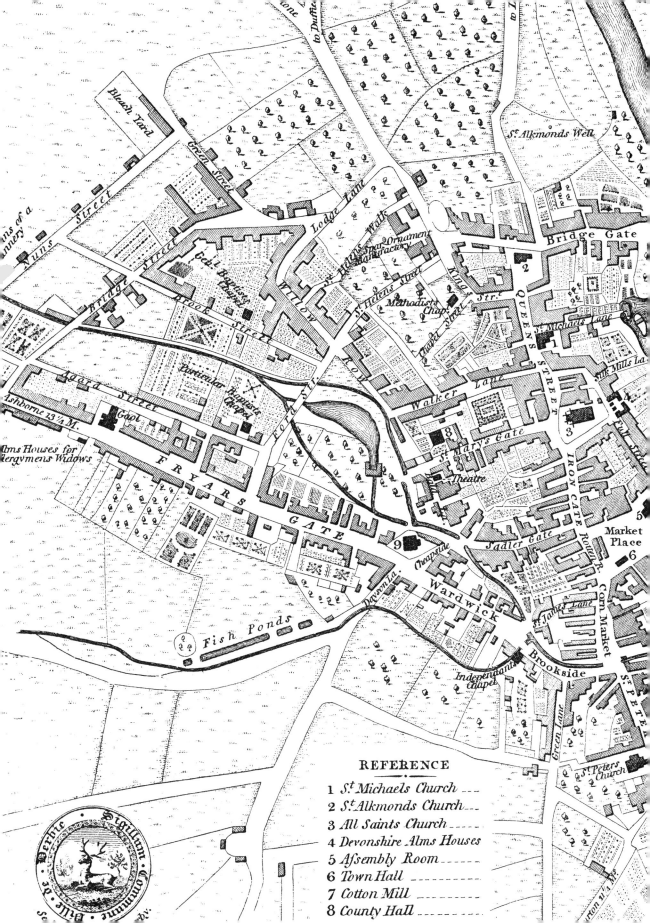

Bleach Yard

Nuns Street

Green Street

Bridge Street

Brook Street

Lodge Lane

Willow Row

St Helens Walk

Genl. Baptists Chapel

Particular Baptists Chapel

Agard Street

Gaol

Alms Houses for Clergymens Widows

Ashborne 13¼ M.

FRYARS GATE

Ford Street

Fish Ponds

Daven La.

Cheapside

Wardwick

St Helens Street

Spar Ornament Manufactory

Methodists Chap.

King's Str.

Chapel Street

Walker Lane

St Mary's Gate

Theatre

Sadler Gate

QUEENS STREET

IRON GATE

St Michaels Lane

Silk Mills La.

Full Street

Royal R.

St James Lane

Corn Market

Green Lane

Independant Chapel

Brookside

St Alkmonds Well

Bridge Gate

St Peters Church

St PETER

Market Place

Sigillum Commune Burgi de Derbie

REFERENCE

1 St Michaels Church ———
2 St Alkmonds Church ———
3 All Saints Church ———
4 Devonshire Alms Houses
5 Assembly Room ———
6 Town Hall ———
7 Cotton Mill ———
8 County Hall ———

Children was established by Dr. Bell in Bold Lane. In order to enter a National School the child had to give evidence of regular attendance at the established church, and be able to recite the Catechism and Creed. In 1831 there were 100 boys and 131 girls at the Bold Lane School. In 1829 another National School was opened by the Reverend Robert Simpson in Traffic Street. The building cost the Rev. Simpson £350 to complete. The school admitted 180 boys and 76 girls. They were taught reading, writing and arithmetic, and the school undertook to furnish them with copy and account books, ink, pens and slates free of charge.

A Lancastrian School for Boys opened in 1812. At first this was in Full Street, but later it moved to a purpose-built school in Orchard Street. Lancastrian Schools were so called because they used a system developed by Joseph Lancaster that trained able pupils to become monitors and instruct younger and less able pupils. The Lancastrian school in Derby was supported by Joseph Strutt who was a personal friend of Lancaster.

By 1831 there were a further three schools in the town. One in Siddalls Lane was also founded by the Reverend Simpson who was a great benefactor to education in the town. For a charge of 2d. a week it educated children aged from two to six years. The infant school in Mill Street charged the same rate, but the Wesleyan Methodist Infant School in Chapel Street charged 3d. a week. In the Wesleyan School the children were instructed through pictures, maps and stories from history and the Bible.

76 *(below)*   Derby from the river in 1875 showing the Shot Tower.

77 *(right)*   Derby Corn Exchange and Shot Tower.

Many of the lessons were in rhyme and either sung or chanted. This method of education was copied from that used by the radical reformer Robert Owen in his school at New Lanark, the village he built for his factory workers. A school especially for girls was opened in 1831. For 1d. a week the girls were taught to sew, keep accounts and read the scriptures.

An important foundation in the early years of the 19th century was the Derby Royal Infirmary. This was built in 1806 and designed by William Strutt in a classical style consisting of a limestone cube of three storeys with a handsome portico supported by Doric pillars backing onto a spacious domed hall. Infectious diseases were admitted

78   Derby Royal Infirmary, designed by William Strutt.

through a side entrance so that they did not mingle with the surgical patients and visitors.

In most early 19th-century hospitals surgical, medical and chronic cases were kept together in one long ward, but the Derby Royal Infirmary was radically different in having small wards of 1-4 beds from the start. Each sex had its own wards which were divided by a unit consisting of a water-closet, scullery and nurses' room. The whole was warm and well ventilated. The DRI, as it is known in the town, could admit 80 patients and was staffed by three physicians, four surgeons, an apothecary and nurses.

The hospital was funded by donations and annual subscriptions from individual benefactors and from parishes. Subscribers had the right to nominate patients according to the amount paid. For £20 a subscriber had the right to nominate one in-patient and six out-patients.

There were strict rules as to what types of patients could be admitted. No domestic servants

were admitted, neither were women over six months pregnant, children under seven, persons with the itch, venereal disease or chronic insanity. Common prostitutes were barred unless they could give evidence that they were reformed characters and all the members of the Trustees of the hospital were agreed that the reformed prostitute should be given a bed.

In the event of every bed being taken a waiting list operated on the following guidelines:

1. First vacant beds to those in greatest need.
2. To those who had applied the week before but had not been admitted.
3. Those living at the greatest distance from the hospital.
4. Those recommended by a subscriber who had not admitted any patients during the previous year.
5. Those recommended by the greatest number of subscribers.

All patients were to be given preference over those with sore legs or those who were chronically sick, or had already been admitted more than twice.

Parish officers who recommended a patient had to supply a two-guinea returnable deposit and, in the case of death, the person who had recommended the patient was responsible for the removal of the corpse from the hospital.

It can be seen that most of the patients being admitted to the hospital depended on patronage or the parish to recommend them. In 1830 a self supporting *Charitable and Parochial Dispensary* was opened in Bridge Street to encourage a free spirit amongst the working classes. Those who could afford it paid 1d. a week towards their medicine, but no one was refused treatment if too poor to contribute. The dispensary also aimed to provide surgical attendance and medicine for poor married women, and paupers who were the most neglected members of society. Finally the dispensary stated that it aimed to 'consult the feelings and promote the comfort of the poor'. Both the dispensary and the infirmary published weekly figures in the *Derby Mercury* of admissions, treatments and those who left the establishments, whether cured or a corpse.[2]

The other source of help for the sick pauper was the workhouse. Prior to the New Poor Law of 1834 each parish had its own workhouse. All Saints' workhouse was built in 1729 and situated in Walker Lane. In 1832 it had 45 inmates. St Alkmund's workhouse was in an ancient building consisting of eight rooms and a bakehouse in Lodge Lane. In 1832 it housed 50 inmates. St Michael's parish was more enlightened. Instead of a workhouse it had a number of parish tenements in St Michael's Lane where it could house whole pauper families rent free. St Peter's workhouse was situated in the parish churchyard and housed 38 persons in 1832.[3]

The respectable aged poor were accom-modated in the numerous almshouses in the town. These included Larges Hospital in Friargate built in 1716 for the widows of poor clergymen. In Bridge Street stood Blacks Almshouses founded in 1630 and home to four poor old men and the same number of women who were required to wear black gowns which gave the charity its name. These almshouses were rebuilt in 1814 by Sir Robert Wilmot. The Liversage charity whose funds had continued to accrue since the 16th-century bequest was probably the most important charity in the town.

Although early 19th-century Derby witnessed the beginnings of modern industrial life, some vestiges of the old traditional ways survived. Public executions still took place, and in 1826 the ducking stool still stood on the west side of the brook by St Werburgh's Church.

The County Hall in St Mary's Gate was rebuilt in 1811, a square building of freestone which still stands today. Its prime function was to house the assizes and contain prisoners during the trials. The prisoners had a 'hole' on the east side of the hall, and there was a large space on the left of the building to accommodate people not involved in the actual trial. There were rooms for Grand and Petty juries and of course a court room. When the hall was opened it contained a marble bust, put up by public subscription to Francis Mundy of Markeaton, a JP for 50 years.

Also built in the early 19th century was the Ordnance Depot. Designed to a plan by James Wyatt, it contained an armoury 75 ft. by 25 ft. which held 15,000 stands of arms. Above this was another room for storing accoutrements for the army. On the north and south sides of the building were the magazines lined with brick for the storage of at least 1,200 barrels of gunpowder. The whole complex created a Midlands depot for the Royal Artillery.[4]

79   The County Hall in St Mary's Gate.

The principle inns of early 19th-century Derby clustered around the central area, and included the *Kings Head*, the *Red* and *White Lions*, the *Tiger* and the *Commercial* in the Cornmarket, the *Bell Inn* in Sadlergate, and the *Royal Oak* in the Market Place. A little further out was the *New Inn* in King Street which housed the royal mail office. The central post office lay in Queen Street with Joseph Bainbridge as its postmaster. The citizens were served by three banks: Messrs. Crompton and Newton in Irongate, Evans and Bingham in St Mary's Gate, and Smith & Co in Rotten Row.

The growth of the commercial area of the town is evidence of increasing prosperity, but this was not spread equally amongst the population, and it was the division between rich and poor that was to spark off riots in the early 19th century. The divide between the prosperous and the poverty stricken in Derby reflected the national situation. Overall the population of the country had grown steadily from 1750 onwards, reaching a peak of growth of 17 per cent between 1811-21. As the population grew it relocated, moving from the countryside to industrial areas to seek work. Population growth in industrial areas outstripped everywhere else and the inflated population of the towns created social problems of overcrowding and bad conditions that the towns were ill equipped to deal with successfully.

At the end of the Napoleonic war in 1815 the situation was exacerbated as demobilised troops returned home to join what was already a swollen labour market. The glut of labour forced down wages, whilst increased demand for commodities, especially food, kept prices high. Despite this a bill excluding the import of cheap foreign corn until home grown corn had reached 80s. a quart was

80 Ordnance Depot designed by James Wyatt.

passed in Parliament in March 1815. This was followed by hunger riots in 1816, and the Staffordshire hunger march.

The agricultural labourers who produced the food gained nothing from the tariff restrictions, and they saw their livelihoods disappearing with the introduction of machinery to farms. In protest they burnt ricks and smashed the machinery in a series of agricultural uprisings which started at Littleport in Cambridgeshire in 1816 and culminated in the Swing Riots that swept the south of the country and some parts of the Midlands in the 1830s.

In the manufacturing areas machines were also seen as taking away the livelihoods of those who worked on the handlooms and stocking frames. Luddite bands broke into mills and factories and destroyed the machinery. In the second and third decade of the 19th century the country was engulfed in flames of protest fanned by starvation and discontent.

The handloom weaver, stocking framer and agricultural labourer had no other means of making their plight known but through direct action. They had no representation in Parliament, and with the suspension of *Habeas Corpus* in 1817 few rights in law. Pressure grew for political reform that would give a more equitable distribution of votes, and allow the working class to have a voice in Parliament and a means of peaceful protest. Political clubs and unions were formed, such as the Hampden Club founded in 1812. These clubs were to provide a platform for the debate on political reform. It was against this background of social deprivation and political excitement that Derby was to be involved in two occurrences of civil disturbance that can be seen as a model for events elsewhere in the country.

The protests over the sale of Nuns Green were peaceful, confined to the pen rather than the sword. But in the early 19th century protests in Derbyshire became more violent. In June 1817 Derby and its population were involved in suppressing the Pentrich Rebellion.

The Pentrich Rebellion took place during a period of intense economic hardship for the labouring poor and especially for the craftsmen who worked in their own homes, such as the stocking framers of the Midlands who produced hosiery for the national market. Exceptionally bad weather in 1816-17 and poor harvests sent up prices, wages could not keep pace with the high prices, whilst many of the workforce were unemployed and depended on poor relief for their sustenance. Such was the dire situation in Derbyshire that in 1817 Sir Henry Fitzherbert noted that at least a third of the working population had become paupers.

In March 1817, 10,000 people had assembled at Manchester each carrying a blanket, intending to march to London to present a petition asking for political reform and help for their plight. In the event most were turned back at Stockport, but about 200 struggled on as far as Ashbourne before giving up. Although the March of the Blanketeers was unsuccessful, it showed the government what a vast number of people the working class could mobilise when necessary. Thus it wanted to make an example of the political clubs and societies that had helped to organise the march, and to show them up as violent and unprincipled organisations in order to frighten away supporters and to stop the movement towards a demand for parliamentary reform. The peaceful protests were suppressed with violence, and the government sent out *agent provocateurs* into the provinces to stir up trouble, and incite the members of the political societies to violence.

Pentrich in Derbyshire was in a hosiery area where the bulk of the workforce were employed in framework knitting. The knitters were led by Jeremiah Brandreth who was 'run' by a government agent named William Oliver, whilst two local informers from Derby, Thomas Bacon and Thomas Turner, who had infiltrated the political societies of the area, kept the local magistrates informed as to what was happening.

Spurred on by the agent, Brandreth formed a plan to overthrow the government by force. In June

1817, 60 men attacked the Butterley Iron Works. Although repulsed, they were quickly joined by 200 men from Codnor, and the two groups set out to march first to Nottingham and then on to London.

Derby was thrown into panic as it was thought that the rebels would attack the town. The mayor called in the 95th regiment to help to defend the town. He also mobilised the Derbyshire Yeomanry, a volunteer mounted regiment.

When the rebels reached Eastwood in Nottinghamshire the troops from Derby and

81 Contemporary drawing of Jeremiah Brandreth the Pentrich rebel.

Nottingham moved against them. The largely unarmed and untrained rebels scattered, and made their way back to their homes as fast as possible. But the ringleaders of the rising, Jeremiah Brandreth, Isaac Ludlam and William Turner were captured and brought to the county gaol in Derby to await their trial.

Such was the interest in the trial by the public that the county hall had to be remodelled to accommodate the sightseers. Instead of being held in the court room the trial was held in the entrance hall of the building. The jury were positioned with their backs to a window so that the light behind them made it difficult for the prisoners to see who they were. It was reported that the prisoners appeared in the dock wearing smock frocks and looking like 'sons of poverty'.

Debate as to the innocence of the prisoners ran high amongst the throng of strangers who had flocked to the town. Many amongst them declared the prisoners innocent dupes and victims of the government's machinations. But the grand jury sworn in for the occasion included all the large local landowners who saw the rebels as a threat to their property and their status in society. Brandreth, Ludlam and Turner were found guilty of treason, and standing at the bar of the court bound by iron shackles they watched the judge don his black cap and declare the fatal words that they were

to be drawn upon a hurdle to the place of execution, and there to be hanged by the neck, and being alive cut down, and your privy members be cut off, and your bowels to be taken out of your belly, and there burned, you being alive; and your head be cut off, and your body to be divided into four quarters and that your head and quarters be disposed of where His Majesty shall think fit.

In the event the sentence was commuted to hanging with beheading to be performed after death. The three prisoners were publicly executed in the county gaol in Derby. The government agent did not give evidence and quietly left the area. Jeremiah Brandreth's wife Ann, who was sent as a pauper back to her home village of Sutton in Ashfield, walked to Derby to see her husband for the last time. She condemned 'that wretch William Oliver' who had drawn her husband in. Before he was executed Jeremiah wrote her a poignant letter of farewell. 'I feel no fear in passing through the shadow of death to eternal life', he wrote, 'so I hope you will make

82 Brandreth as a convicted traitor was symbolically beheaded after his death by hanging.

the promise of God as I have, to your own soul as we may meet in Heaven. My beloved.' He sent her his workbag which he had carried with him during the rising. It contained two balls of worsted and one of cotton, a handkerchief, an old pair of stockings and a shirt.[5]

The Pentrich rebellion made no difference to the condition of the poor, nor to their representation in Parliament. Fourteen years later with the introduction of the Reform Bill into Parliament it looked as if there would be a more equitable distribution of votes amongst the electorate. Although it was not the intention of the bill to give the vote to the labourer or pauper, the leaders of the working class played on the hopes of the poor that better conditions would follow for them if the bill was passed. Radical writers such as William Cobbett led the labourer to believe that if the bill was passed the labourer and pauper would get cottages and land of their own, and bread for their children. There was great excitement as the bill went through Parliament. Such was the excitement in Derby that a special messenger was hired to gallop in a chaise pulled by a relay of horses to bring the news to the town of the final vote on the bill.

The final vote on the bill took place on Friday, 7 October 1831. On 8 October a large and highly excited crowd gathered in the market place to hear the news. The tired messenger arrived at the Guildhall and delivered his news—that the bill had failed on its final vote. A muffled peal of bells was rung from the parish churches in order to alert those at the back of the vast crowd as to what had happened. For a moment there was silence as the crowd absorbed the news. Then it began to react. Anger swept through its ranks. Stones were thrown at William Bemrose's printing shop which stood in the market place. Bemrose was an anti-reformer, and had displayed a petition against the bill in his shop window. Once the first stone was thrown it was followed by others. Very soon every window in the shop was broken and the shop gutted. Bemrose was to claim compensation of £7,712 from the corporation for damages. The crowd moved on to the shop of another printer, Henry Mosley. All the glass in Mosley's shop was broken. At this point a gentlemen, William Baker, who was known to be a pro-reformer, tried to reason with the mob and stop the violence. But the crowd were now too excited to listen and continued on their way. They broke the windows of Thomas Cox's house, and attacked the residence of the Rev. Charles Stead Hope. The Church was targeted in the Reform Bill riots everywhere because the Bishops in the House of Lords were against the bill.

Other targets were the gaols, and the landed gentry. After attacking the house of the governor of the county gaol, the Derby mob divided into three. One group marched to Markeaton Hall and pulled up palings and shrubs in the park. Another group continued to Kedleston Hall, where a cannon was aimed at them but not fired. A third party went to Chaddesden Hall.

The riot died down in the small hours of the night of 9 October. The next morning many of the rioters returned to the market place where they demanded the release of two persons arrested during the disturbance of the previous night. When this was refused the rioters marched on to the borough gaol to release them by force. They uprooted a lamp post and used it to batter the gaol door down, and release the 23 prisoners inside. After this success the rioters continued to the county gaol in order to

83 *(left)* Late 19th-century drawing of the Guildhall and market place where the crowd gathered to hear the result of the vote on the Reform Bill in 1831.

84 *(below)* Contemporary account of the crowd's reception of the news that the Reform Bill had failed to get through Parliament.

An account of the important news brought by the London mail this Evening, of Earl of Grey's visit to the King, when his Majesty expressed his full determination to stand true to the Reform Cause, and and to prorogue the Parliament immediately; likewise an account of a motion carried in the House of Commons, to stand true to the Reform Bill. Also an account of an attack which was made on Lord Londonderry.

The London Courier of this evening states, that Earl Grey and the other Ministers had an interview with his Majesty, at which the utmost cordiality and unanimity prevailed, and a determination to persevere in the measure of Reform. A propagation of Parliament was to take place on Friday or Saturday. Lord Ebrington brought forward a motion in the House of Commons, which was carried by a majority of one hundred and thirty one, by which the House pledged itself to support his Majesty and his Ministers in the plan of Reform which had been passed the House. The same paper states, that a number of the Lords and Bishops are already repenting of the votes they gave, and that they will vote for the Reform Bill; the next time it is brought before the House.—London Paper.

Attack on the Marquis of Londonderry (Lord Castlereagh's brother Lord Londonderry stated to the House of Lords that he had been attacked and nearly pulled out of his cabriolet by riotous men. An attack had been made on his house last night, and had he had his windows mended since his house was last attacked, they would have been again all broken.

(From the Glasgow Chronicle of Oct. 12.)

Derby, Oct. 8. [1831

I was interrupted in writing to you last night by the most dreadful yells, followed by the noise of violence, and on going to the end of the Street, found an immense concourse of people collected in front of Mr Mozely's house, (formerly occupied by mrs Henley); he is an extensive printer, and though his name was Henry, the mob identified him as the Anti-Reform correspondent of Lord Londonderry. After an hour's crashing and shouting, every pane of glass in the windows was broken, and demolished, of which I was a witness till ten o'clock. The news arrived in Derby (of the rejection of the bill) by six o'clock, by messengers belonging to a London newspaper, in a chaise & four.—The mob have demolished the front of Mr. Hope's house, as well of the Anti-Reform printer, Bemrose, in the Market Place, and much injured Mr. Laken, the Town Clerk. The mob afterwards went to Mr Monday's, at markeaton, and destroyed the windows. They afterwards went to Chaddesden and committed the same injury to the property of the family of Wilton.—The Town Jail has been broken open, and an escape of prisoners taken place. The mob are now attacking the County Jail which a small party are defending,—They have fired from the roof, killed one man, and wounded several others. I have not time to write any more.

It is lamentable that such scenes should take place at a period like the present, when every thing should be refrained from which would give the enemies of the people the least cause to triumph and make a handle of. Patience, in the greatest extremity, has often produced the desired effect, and will ultimately do so in the issue of the Reform Bill,

The Sun London newspaper says that Nottingham Castle, the property of the Duke of Newcastle has been burned to the ground.

John Muir, printer

release those incarcerated there. But the governor was ready for them and had positioned armed men positioned on the roof. He gave the order and they fired into the crowd, hitting a youth named Garner in the stomach, and wounding three others. At this point Sir Charles Colville, the High Sheriff of the county, and Thomas Gisburne MP appeared on the scene, and managed to disperse the mob with promises that they would ensure that the bill would be re-presented in Parliament in the near future.

The mob retired for a while, but then reformed and marched to Chester Green where they smashed the glass in the windows and doors of Mr. Harrison's house. They re-entered the borough across St Mary's Bridge, where they wrenched off the coping stones to use as ammunition.

They marched back towards the town centre demolishing street lamps and smashing the windows and shutters of houses as they went. Damage was inflicted in Friargate, Irongate, Queen Street, Duffield Road, Lodge Lane and in the market place. Henry Haden, a surgeon who attempted to remonstrate with the mob in Irongate, was thrust to the ground. When attempts were made to raise him he was found to be dead. The subsequent inquest on him revealed that he died from natural causes precipitated by his rough treatment at the hands of the mob. He is buried in the nave of All Saints' Church where there is a memorial to him on the south wall.

Unsubdued, the mob tore up the palings around All Saints' and attacked the post office. Rioting continued through Sunday night. On Monday morning the mob returned again to the market place to be met by the mayor. He promised that if they would disperse he would sent a petition to Parliament asking them to reconsider the bill. Specially printed handbills were distributed amongst the crowd stating the mayor's proposals. But by this time the mob were no longer politically motivated but more interested in destruction. They smashed six market stalls set up by traders, and threw the pieces about.

Fearing the worst the mayor had sent to Nottingham for help from the military, and the 15th Hussars were standing by ready for action. As the mob seemed intent on another orgy of destruction the mayor read the Riot Act. Once the Riot Act was read anyone on the street could be cleared off by force, and all rioters summarily arrested. The Hussars with sabres drawn quickly cleared the market place, injuring several rioters in the process. One, John Kay, who was injured by a sabre cut in the thigh, subsequently claimed for loss of earnings from the Sheffield-based friendly society to which he belonged. Tragically a by-stander John Hickling was shot dead whilst watching proceedings from the doorway of the *Greyhound* inn.

The mob fled up Duffield road and continued on their destructive course until the Hussars, reinforced by the Radbourne, Burton and Leicestershire Yeomanries, restored order. By Tuesday, 11 October the town was quiet again.

Eleven persons were arrested and charged with felony and breaking into the borough gaol. All of those arrested were young males: William Hudson (aged 29), John Roome (20), Thomas Roberts (29), Francis Bamford (20), George Mossdale (22), William Walter (20), John Hanson (21), Luke Needham (28), James Wardle (32) and Samuel Kish (20). One woman, Catherine Henrys, aged 23, was also arrested, and the authorities advertised for information about another woman named Sherwin who had been seen

85 'Mourn for Reform' a ballad produced after the failure of the Reform Bill.

MOURN
For REFORM.
A new Song wrote on the late riots at London Nottingham, and Derby, where houses were burnt and lives lost,

Come all you just reformers
　Wherever you may be,
I pray you give attention
　And listen unto me :
The fate of our reform bill
　As you shall understand
Was thrown out by their lordships
　With an unsparing hand.
　　CHORUS.
　Britains all now lets mourn
　For king William and reform.

And what have their great lordships
　gain'd
　By heeding not our moan ;
The hatred of all right good men,
　And the envy of none.
The people all cry out amain
　Lets have a just reform ;
Nor heed the boroughmongering train,
　Who hollow out forlorn.

Earl Grey has firmly stated,
　The helm he'll not quit,
Then while the King and he hath
　sworn,
　Or on one stone hath spit ;
Reformers will take heart I pray,
　And still united be,
Avoid excess of every kind,
　And yet wait patiently.

The Chancellor, Lord Brougham the
　brave,
　Stands resolute and firm,
And treats the Bishops at arm's length,
　With pity and with scorn,
Lord Warncliff has declared that he
　Now sees it must be so ;
And Londonderry's Marquis has
　Received a knock down blow,

At Derby they've been very wild,
　And broke the windows all,
And three have lost their precious lives
　By powder and with ball ;
They've broke the gaol doors open wide
　And let the culprits out,
Who soon did join, mischief to do,
　With a tremendous shout.

In spite of all the priest could do,
　Whose mind was on the rack,
At Birmingham they toll'd the bells,
　And hung the church with black :
At Nottingham the castle of
　The great Newcastle duke,
Was burnt unto the ground full soon,
　Which had an awfull look.

The king has said unto the trades,
　Of the great London town,
Be firm, be strong and all unite,
　To put the riots down :
And on Our word Reform you'll get,
　Which happiness will bring,
So to conclude lets shout aloud
　God bless our patriot king.

Stephenson Printer Gateshead.

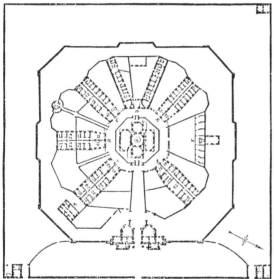

86 *(above)*   The new county gaol in Vernon Street, later used as a greyhound stadium.

87 *(left)*   The plan of the gaol shows it to follow the utilitarian ideas of Jeremy Bentham who designed an ideal prison to this plan.

The claims suggest that little actual looting took place. Only two claimants sued for loss of property. This included a book, an overcoat and a pair of silver spectacles.

Although the riots died away, the feeling of unrest in the town continued in the following weeks. On 18 October 1831 the town clerk reported that, although the town was quiet, the working class had not yet returned to their occupations. However on 25 October the mayor considered that the town was sufficiently peaceful to order the withdrawal of the troops.[6]

Events in Derby following the defeat of the Reform Bill were replicated across the country. In Nottingham rioters besieged Wollaton Hall, and at Bristol the mob controlled the town for three days.

The Reform Bill eventually passed through Parliament in 1832. Again a great concourse gathered in the Market Place, but this time the bells pealed joyfully across the town reporting the success of the bill. A procession of pro-reformers passed peacefully through the town, led by respectable tradesmen who had supported the bill from the start but had avoided involvement in the violence that had followed its earlier defeat.

Although the militia were on stand-by a decade later when the corporation endeavoured to suppress the Shrovetide Football Match, the Reform Bill riots

carrying stones in St Mary's Gate. Other witnesses came forward and named rioters they had observed damaging property, but they were not arrested. All but two of those apprehended were acquitted which throws some doubt as to the severity of the riots, and suggests some exaggeration in the contemporary accounts of the events.

Those whose property had been damaged sued the corporation for failing to take adequate precautions to prevent the riot and damage. In all there were 37 claims for damages, mostly for smashed windows. Invoices attached to the claims show that replacing the square panes in the elegant Georgian town houses of Friargate cost from 3s. 6d. to 5s. 6d. per pane.

mark the end of violent action by the crowd in Derby. In the second half of the 19th century protests were structured, organised by trade unionists, or by moral reformers such as those who marched against the Sunday opening of the post office in 1868.

The maintenance of law and order became less dependent on special constables and the military when Derby Corporation Police Force was founded in 1836. This consisted of eight men and 10 nightwatchmen—a uniformed and professional body of men charged with keeping law and order in the borough.

Wrongdoers were kept either in the borough or the county gaol. The borough gaol had been moved out to the Nuns Green area in the 18th century where William Hutton observed wryly that he had seen the jailer himself confined for playing football which the mayor Isaac Borrow was determined to suppress. From Nuns Green the borough gaol moved to Willow Row and then to the Kensington area.[7]

The county gaol in Friargate was rebuilt on land belonging to Larges Hospital in 1827. This was one of the finest specimens of gaol architecture in the county. Built in a classical mode, it had an impressive entrance. It could house 90 prisoners, and the accommodation included a tread mill. Two hundred and seventy prisoners were admitted in 1830, but usually there were only 40 people present at any one time, and the gaol only became seriously overcrowded when prisoners were delivered from outside the town for their trials at the assizes. Debtors remained steady at an average of 50 prisoners a year.

Long-term imprisonment was not seen as a viable option in the early 19th century. Those who were not released after a few months were either destined to be hung or transported to the colonies.

88 The Piazzas in the Market Place shortly before demolition.

Between the years 1815-31, 144 prisoners from Derby were transported to the colonies for life, and a further 202 for seven years. In 1857 transportation for life was replaced by penal servitude and longer gaol sentences. This was considered to be a more humanitarian punishment than transportation or hanging.[8]

In 1841 the population had risen to 32,741. As well as growing larger with developments filling in the space between Ashbourne and Kedleston roads, and spreading along the London and Normanton roads, the town was also changing. After a severe flood in 1842 the Markeaton brook was culverted. A little later St Peter's Street and Irongate were widened, and the market place altered with the removal of the covered piazzas. But the biggest change that happened to the town in the early 19th century was of course the coming of the railways.

Chapter Nine

Railways and Entertainment—
Derby in the mid-19th Century

At the start of the 1830s Derby was in the grip of a trade depression which contemporary observers such as the editor of the *Derby Mercury* attributed to the fact that, whereas other towns had acquired links that meant goods could be transported quickly and cheaply across the country, Derby lagged behind in this development. In 1832 the first railway line in the Midlands was opened between Leicester and Swannington. This gave Leicester easy access to coal from the Leicestershire coalfield, and removed a valuable market from the east Derbyshire collieries. Worried colliery owners and traders started to clamour for a railway line in Derbyshire as well. A group of coal owners met at the *Sun Inn* in Eastwood, Nottinghamshire and decided that they would invest in a railway company to be called the Midland Counties Railway Company. The first shareholders included local landowners such as Edward Mundy, and Messrs. Haslam. Their aim was to link the Derbyshire coalfield with Leicester and to run a branch line to Derby.

A public meeting held in Derby Town Hall on 2 December 1835 was attended by over 2,000 people including most of the town's manufacturers and tradesmen. They voted unanimously to support by petitions any bills put into Parliament that would bring the railways to Derby. The *Derby Mercury* reported the proceedings of the meeting, adding that railways from Leeds to Derby, and Derby to Birmingham would make 'Derby the central point of communication between North and South, and the Southwest of England which must be highly advantageous to trade and manufacturers of the town, and therefore is intitled to the warmest support of its inhabitants'.[1]

Although there are parallels between the extension of the railways to the town and the introduction of turnpike roads and the canal system in the 18th century, in that the clamour for these developments started when it seemed as if the town's trade would suffer if it was left out of advances in the transport infra-structure, there are also important differences. The initiative for the formation of the Midland Counties railway company was local, but other companies interested in Derby came from outside the area. Furthermore, investment in the companies included a large number of shareholders from outside the locality, and the whole undertaking was on a much larger scale than the earlier developments in transport. The projected lines which focused on Derby were part of a general trend towards the establishment of long trunk lines linking provincial centres with each other, and with London. These projects required a huge capital investment and, like the canal companies, the shareholders had to wait before they realised any profit from their investment.

Three railway companies were interested in opening lines to the town: the Midland Counties, the North Midland Railway Company, and the Birmingham and Derby Junction Railway Company. The North Midland was launched from York by George Hudson, the 'Railway King' who aimed to control all traffic coming from London to the north east, and from the north east to the south west of the country. Local investors in the North Midland included William Leaper Newton, alderman and sometime mayor of the borough, who was also on the corporation's special railway committee.

Sir Robert Peel whose family home was at Tamworth, and Sir Oswald Mosley from Rolleston in Staffordshire were the prime movers behind the Birmingham and Derby Junction Railway Company.

In 1836 Parliamentary Acts were passed which allowed for railway lines to be run into Derby from

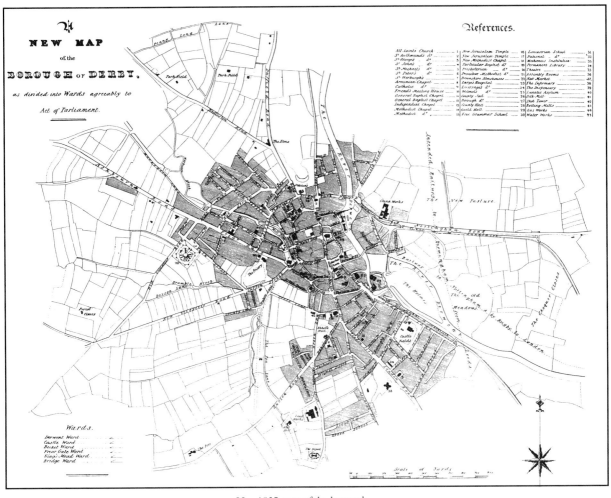

89 1835 map of the borough.

Nottingham and Birmingham, whilst the North Midland Railway Company would connect Derby directly to London. Usually in the 19th century each railway company had its own station as close to the town centre as possible. At first the Midland Counties proposed to terminate its line in Derby on a piece of land owned by William Eaton Mousley contiguous to the Derwent by Exeter Bridge, known as Darby's yard. The North Midland wanted its terminus on Nottingham Road. However, by November 1835 the railway companies had realised that a shared station would be a more economically viable solution. The estates committee of the corporation had reached the same conclusion. At a council meeting held in February 1836 Mr. Johnson, the chairman of the estates committee, pointed out the desirability of the companies making their station

on The Holmes, and a deputation was sent from the council to George Stephenson, the North Midland's engineer, to propose this. The suggestion was rejected by the companies who considered that the site was too low lying and would be subject to flooding, and asked instead for land on Castlefields. The council retaliated by withholding permission for the companies to cross corporation land in the town. Eventually in 1838 the impasse was resolved when the corporation agreed to allow the companies to purchase land on Castlefields, and to improve access to The Holmes.

How far either the companies or the council were motivated by social concerns, and how far by economic is difficult to ascertain. Undoubtedly a shared station sited away from the town centre was environmentally friendly, and eliminated the

90   The station designed by Francis Thompson for the railway companies that united to form the Midland Railway Company.

devastation and pollution that would have followed if three stations had been constructed, but there was some economic gain to the town. The railway companies had to purchase the customary rights in the Old Meadows and The Holmes, and William Leaper Newton who lived in Castlefields House sold this for a profit. It is also possible that George Hudson was already contemplating the amalgamation of the three companies, and saw that a joint station at Derby, lying at the hub of his proposed national network, would provide the nucleus of his rail empire, and encouraged the companies to agree to a shared station. Opening up a virgin site in Litchurch helped to stimulate trade as cabs, omnibuses and carriers were needed to transport passengers and goods from the town centre out to the station.[2]

Francis Thompson, the North Midland company's architect, designed the station. The designs were ready to go out to tender in 1839. The tender was won by Thomas Jackson of Pimlico who offered to build Derby a station for £39,986. The two smaller companies, the Birmingham and Derby Company and the Midland Counties, were to pay £4,796 and £4,925 respectively, and a rent of six

per cent a year to use the station, whilst the larger North Midland would pay the rest. The running and maintenance of the North Midland was controlled by George and Robert Stephenson, and it was an experienced and prestigious company.

The station façade was 1,050 ft. long. It opened on to a glazed train shed 34 ft. high with the roof held on cast-iron columns. Originally it was designed as one long platform inter-sected by turntables. Later this idea was abandoned in favour of separate platforms. As work started on the station it also began on the *Midland Hotel* which Francis Thompson designed as well, and on the workshops and engine sheds. The station opened in May 1840 and was described by one observer as a 'market place for steam'. In 1844 the three companies amalgamated to become the Midland Railway Company.

Originally each company had its own workshops and round houses with turntables to turn the engines. The North Midland's round house had 16 lines leading to a central turntable with space for two engines per line. There were at least 16 engines in steam daily at the Derby depot. The early North

91   Interior view of the station.

Midland engines were the Robert Stephenson long boiler or hay box type locomotives.

It was research into the design and production of new and more efficient locomotives which was to make the Derby yards famous. In 1851 the first locomotive designed and built at Derby was produced. It was number 147, a six-wheeled goods tender. By 1855, 33 engines had been built at Derby and in 1857 the first section of steel rather than iron track on the whole of the British railway network was laid at the north end of Derby station, where heavy traffic meant that iron rails needed replacing every six months.

The superintendent of the new amalgamated Midland Railway Company was Matthew Kirtley who had been trained by Robert Stephenson. He received a salary of £250 a year. His elder brother, Thomas, who had also worked in the Derby yards, stayed on as an inspector before moving on to the Brighton, Chatham and South Eastern railway. Thomas's son, William, was to return to Derby as workshop superintendent, and there was a strong tradition of family connections at the Midland Railway Company. It was Matthew Kirtley who worked on the first locomotive built in the works, using the skills of local engineering works such as Andrew Handyside's Britannia foundry to help him. Handysides were to produce all the iron work for the Midland Railway stations, and the bridges over the lines. Their work includes the magnificent span of the roof over St Pancras's station in London. Handysides foundry was established in 1815. Handysides also worked on Amsterdam's central station. As well as railway architecture it specialised in making street furniture such as lamp posts and letter boxes. Examples of the latter can be seen in forgotten corners of the old British Empire.

Experimental work was to continue in the Derby locomotive shops. In 1859 Frederick Smith,

92   Examples of Handyside letter boxes from a pattern book sent to prospective customers.

93   Matthew Kirtley's obelisk in the Uttoxeter New Road Cemetery. Its inscription reads:'This monument was erected by the employes [*sic*] of the locomotive and carriage departments as a token of their affection ...'.

one of the Midland's longest established drivers, drove the first of a new type of engine tender which burnt cheaper bituminous coal rather than the more expensive coke used before. This development was the result of work by Charles Markham, the outdoor locomotive superintendent, known in the works as 'Longstockings'.[3]

Matthew Kirtley worked with the Midland until his death at his home Litchurch Grange in 1873. He was buried in the Uttoxeter New Road Cemetery. His grave is marked by a marble obelisk paid for by contributions from his fellow workers at the Midland. On his death the company possessed 1,012 engines.

Kirtley was followed by Samuel Waite Johnson as superintendent. One of the changes Johnson was to make was to change the dark green livery favoured by Kirtley to the deep crimson lake which still identifies Midland stock. Johnson was to stay with the Midland until his retirement in 1903. Ironically,

shortly after his retirement the man who had walked across main lines without harm was run down by a horse and trap in Nottingham and killed.

As well as designing the *Midland Hotel*, Francis Thompson also designed a complex of cottages and other buildings for the railway's workmen and their families, which were built in 1842 at the company's expense on the land opposite the station frontage. These were good quality substantial two-storied houses built of red brick, standing on a stone plinth with key stones on the windows, and stone cornerstones or quoins to add interest to the design.

Litchurch where the railway was situated grew from a tiny hamlet containing 35 people in 1801 to a large village with a population of 6,560 in 1861. The Midland Railway Company provided the township with Sunday Schools, a church, clubs such as a rowing club and a public house, *The Brunswick Inn*. It was here in 1851 that the workers formed a reading society which was to grow into the Derby Railway Institute where free adult education was provided. Although the railway community quickly had its own identity, its presence was felt in the rest of the town as well. A steam whistle known as the 'Loco Bull' marked the beginning and end of shifts, and many townspeople set their watches by it. When its operator inadvertently sounded the whistle at noon rather than one o'clock confusion followed throughout the town.

The Midland Railway Company were pater-nalistic employees caring for the mental, physical and spiritual welfare of their workers, but they were also strict about the behaviour of their workforce and dismissed anyone heard swearing, seen fighting or committing a breach of working regulations. Nevertheless, workers stayed with the Midland for the whole of their working lives. One locomotive driver, Joseph Pickering, worked for the company from 1845 to 1882 and on his retirement wrote to the company suggesting that they might like to pay him a pension. They declined to do this.

As well as engine drivers, firemen, porters and the other staff required to run a Victorian railway system, the Midland also employed two official photographers, Thomas Scotton and his son Thomas Albert. They made a pictorial record of the station, rolling stock and workshops as well as taking pictures of Derbyshire scenery for brochures advertising the

94 Railway cottages designed by Francis Thompson for the Midland Railway company.

railway, and prints that were framed and placed in every compartment of the passenger trains. The National Railway Museum in York holds the collection of glass negatives from the Midland Railway Company, but much of the surviving early rolling stock can be seen at the Midland Railway Centre at Butterley in Derbyshire.

The Midland Railway Company was not above meddling in politics. In 1848 their support for the Conservative candidate in the general election led to a commons inquiry into the 'railway interest' in politics.

The railway not only facilitated the transport of goods but also stimulated trade throughout the town. Handyside's Britannia Foundry was just one of the firms that benefited. William Bemrose the printer won the contract to print the Midland's timetables and stationery, and on his own initiative Bemrose produced an annual series of *Red Books* packed with information about Derby and its railways for inhabitants and visitors. The clothing industry also revived with the demand for uniforms

from the station staff. Heavy engineering firms were attracted by the cheap carriage of goods offered by the railway and the easy access from Derby to raw materials such as iron and coal, and set up works and foundries beside the railway lines. Sir Francis Ley's Vulcan Foundry is an example of this. Thus it can be seen that the editor of the *Derby Mercury* was correct in his assumption that the railway would be

95 Contemporary cartoon on the railway influence on the 1848 general election.

96 William Bemrose, a member of the printing firm which won the contract to print the Midland Railway company's stationery.

advantageous to trade in the town and be of mutual benefit to all.

Thanks to the foresight of the town council the centre of the town remained intact until the 1870s when the Great Northern Railway planned a route which would link Uttoxeter, Derby and Nottingham to the Erewash valley. This company was not interested in sharing the existing station but wanted a prestigious building in the centre of town. This time the town council had no objections and granted them permission to build a station in Friargate. The line was opened in 1878, and it radically altered Derby's townscape, bringing pollution, noise and congestion right into the heart of the town. It destroyed houses and much valuable archaeological evidence.

The line entered the town from the north-east cutting directly through the Roman fort of *Derventio*. It was then carried on a high embankment and iron bridges through Little Chester where the occupants were forced to live under a pall of smoke, and in the shadows of embankments. The line crossed

the Derwent on an iron bridge built by Handyside which is now used as a footbridge. From there it went under North Parade, Edward and King streets in a cutting, and crossed the area between King Street and Friargate on a bridge supported on high brick arches. At Friargate the line crossed the road on another Handyside bridge. Here, as befitted the area, it was an elegant structure with filigree decoration enclosing the stag from the Derby coat of arms. In order that traffic could pass underneath this bridge a dip was made in the road which frequently flooded.

On the south side of Friargate the Great Northern Railway built a large station with raised platforms, and a complex of large red-brick warehouses. The engine sheds were built on what is now Great Northern Road, and the line continued across the area on red brick arches beside the Old Uttoxeter Road and then on to Mickleover and westwards to Uttoxeter.

The GNR changed the face of much of the town. South Street was destroyed entirely, including the medieval Eyre's House, and the *Old White Horse Inn*. Some areas were turned into wastelands that have never recovered. However, the line increased

97 Great Northern Railway's bridge over the Derwent, designed and built by Handysides. This is now a footbridge.

98 Great Northern Railway's bridge over Friargate, also designed and built by Handysides.

99 Great Northern Railway's warehouses in Great Northern Road.

the town's reliance on the railways for employment. In 1862 over 2,000 people were employed by the railway companies; this had risen to 4,000 by 1892.

Not only did railways change the townscape, but they also changed people's lives. Faster, cheaper transport meant that it was no longer necessary for everyone to live close to where they worked but enabled them to commute into town from the villages on the outskirts, such as Duffield and Mickleover.

The railways also encouraged those who had not previously travelled to explore further afield, taking advantage of the special excursion trains the railway companies ran. The general public first sampled the delights of rail travel during the Great Exhibition of 1851 when whole villages travelled by train to London. In August 1871 the first ever bank holiday Monday occurred. Almost the entire population of Derby left the town to take special excursion trains to the countryside or the sea. For many this was the first paid holiday they had ever taken, although the railway companies themselves had been giving their workers a week's paid holiday each year by that date.

Not only did the 19th-century worker have little opportunity for leisure, but the increase in the size of the town and the infilling of open spaces with houses, such as the development between Ashbourne and Kedleston roads, meant that there were few places left where the worker could walk at leisure or play games. Often the public house or tavern was the only place of recreation for the working classes.

In 1828 an attempt had been made by Dr. Douglas Fox and Joseph and Edward Strutt to

remedy this by the foundation of the Mechanics Institute which was intended to be a working and lower middle-class version of the Philosophical Society. At its start the Mechanics Institute offered free lectures to 'artisans and those of limited education so that they might improve their knowledge'. In 1829 it had a membership of 274. This rose steadily to 2,000 in 1842. By that time the institute had a purpose-built lecture room and a library of 6,000 books. The improving lectures were still available, but were no longer free for all. Members of the institute had free admission to the back seats and the gallery but paid 3d. for the front seats, whilst the general public could attend the lectures for the payment of 6d. a seat at the front and 3d. at the back. Examples of the programme of lectures included a series on forensic medicine in 1834, and on 29 March 1855 a lecture by Mrs. Clara Balfour on 'The Intellectual Influence of Women in Society'.

Another attempt to provide both leisure and education was the opening of the Arboretum in 1840. The Arboretum was given to the town by the generosity of Joseph Strutt who not only donated 11 acres of land to the town, but also hired the well-known gardener John Claudius Loudon to design a park for him. He created a park which was a complex of small hillocks and gravelled walks between beds in which rare trees and shrubs were planted. Each plant bore a label with its Latin and English names so that exercise could be combined with education.

The Arboretum opened with three days of celebration on 16, 17 and 18 September 1840. Each day was designated for a different section of society. The first was for the mayor and the town's élite at which the mayor officially received the park as a gift for the town. As well as speeches and ceremonies the programme included dancing, promenades and musical entertainments. The second day was for the tradesmen and included a procession of floats sponsored by tradesmen and local societies which set out for the park from Friargate. The third day was children's day, with games and dancing. Until 1882 visitors had to pay to enter the Arboretum which limited access to the better off, but in 1882 the park was made free to all, provided that they were decently dressed.

Joseph Strutt's example was followed by Michael Thomas Bass who gave the town a recreation

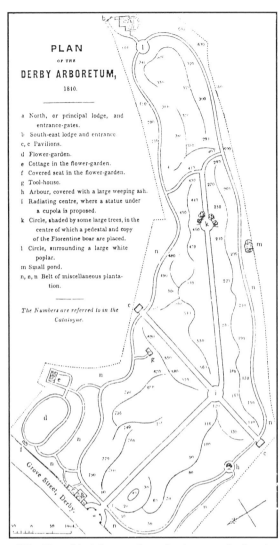

100 Plan of the Arboretum from a book presented to Joseph Strutt when the park opened.

101 A late 19th-century drawing of the fountain in the Arboretum. Other items of interest in the park included a bandstand and the statue of a wild boar.

ground in 1867, and in 1873 added to it an open air swimming pool. The Mundys of Markeaton also generously gave land in 1895, for a park to the west of the town and Osmaston Park opened on land owned by the Wilmot family in 1922. This was followed in 1929 by Darley Park which was developed on land owned by the Evans family which

102 Michael Thomas Bass, Liberal M.P. and benefactor to the town.

had previously been part of Darley Abbey. Another Evans house and grounds, Allestree Park, became a public park and municipal golf course in 1948.

All of the parks provided some form of recreational exercise, such as tennis, bowls and rowing, but what really interested the working class in 19th-century Derby was football. Not just any football game, but the traditional Shrovetide football match; a chaotic and exuberant game which involved the whole town, with goals at Nuns Mill in the north and the Gallows Balk in the south of the town, and in which much of the action took place in the Derwent or Markeaton brook. Nominally the players came from All Saints' and St Peter's parishes, but in practice the game was a free for all with as many as 1,000 players. A Frenchman who observed the match in 1829 wrote in horror, 'if Englishmen call this play, it would be impossible to say what they call fighting'.

The game started at 2 o'clock when the pancake bells were rung. A 19th-century pamphlet gives the following rhyme which was chanted as the bells rang out:

> Pancakes and fritters
> Say All Saints and St Peters
> When will the ball come?
> Say the bells of St Alkmun's;
> At two they will throw
> Says St Werabo
> O! very well
> Says little St Michael![4]

The ball, which was made of leather stuffed with cork shavings, was thrown to the assembled players in the market place. Players were usually stripped to the waist and every effort was made by fair means or foul to score a goal. Cheating was rife, and on one occasion the ball was un-stuffed and its components smuggled through the crowds under a woman's dress to be reassembled by the rival's goal. When a goal was scored the bells of the jubilant parish rang out.

For two days each year on Shrove Tuesday and Ash Wednesday the town was taken over by this mêlée, with loss of trade, damage to property and an increase in petty crime. Such was the disruption to the life of the town, the threat to public order and individual morals that in 1845 the town council decided to ban the match for once and for all. It offered instead a sports day with prizes, to be held on The Holmes. Competitions such as jumping matches, blindfold foot races and sack races for which each participant was to bring his own sack were to be held, as well as other entertainments. On Ash Wednesday boys could take part in a plum pudding and treacle eating match or swarm up a greasy pole to bring down a joint of meat.

The council warned that the prizes would not be awarded if any football was played on the streets during the sports days and as a substitute it organised a knock-out football competition for local teams with a prize of £10 for the winners. The aim of the sports was to 'promote a social and kindly feeling ... to give a fair field for manly exercises and innocent relations free from all immorality and vicious excitement'. It was felt that much of the immorality and vicious excitement was caused by the demon drink, so liqueur was banned from The Holmes, and anyone caught spoiling the entertainment was to be held up to public ridicule and tossed up in a blanket.

In the event many townsfolk ignored the official sports and tried to hold the football match in the streets as usual. They were stopped by the borough police augmented from outside, with the military on standby. By the following Shrove Tuesday the council had passed a byelaw forbidding the match, and attempts to revive it during the 19th century were not successful.[5]

Shrovetide football matches were traditional all over the country, and probably date back to pagan times. Usually the teams were representatives of ancient rivalries from different areas of a town, and the ball used was sometimes an inflated bladder, but could also be a barrel or the carcase of an animal thrown into the crowd by a local dignitary. Ashbourne in Derbyshire is one of the few places where the Shrovetide football match still takes place.

Participation in football as an organised game continued in Derby, with numerous works, churches and society teams playing each other. But it is with the development of the Derbyshire County Cricket Club and the Derby County Football Club that we see the emergence of commercialised spectator sport. Cricket had been played in the county since at least 1757. The town had its own cricket team by 1792 when it played Castle Donington. In 1823 there were several cricket clubs in the town such as the Derby Old Club, the Derby Independents and the Derby Town Club. In 1824 the South Derbyshire Cricket Club moved from Chaddesden to The Holmes with an inaugural match against an All-England eleven. The club moved to the Racecourse ground in 1863, and in 1870 the Derbyshire County Cricket Club was formed. Its first captain and club secretary was Sam Richardson, a gentleman's outfitter. In 1889 he absconded to Spain taking £1,000 of the club's money with him. Eventually he became a court tailor to King Alfonso, and died in Spain at the age of 93 in 1938.

The club was dominated from 1874-84 by William Mycroft, a powerful left-arm bowler, and in the 1890s by England batsman William Storer,

DERBY SHROVETIDE SPORTS, 1845.

In the Town of Derby a practice prevailed for a great length of time to play at Foot Ball in the public streets and thoroughfares on Shrove Tuesday, which led to a similar practice within the last half century on Ash Wednesday, and though such practices were illegal, whilst the Town contained only few inhabitants but little inconvenience was sustained, and they were assented to, until they have become a great public nuisance and a source of much private injury. The authorities of the Town have therefore found it necessary, whenever any complaint shall be made, to carry into effect the law, which several modern Acts of Parliament have provided the means of doing, at comparatively little trouble and expense.

Under such circumstances it is understood that such persons as might otherwise have played at Foot Ball as heretofore will not attempt to do so, and as many inhabitants are desirous that there should be other Sports, a handsome Subscription has been entered into to provide Sports for the present and future years.

The following are Sports selected for the present year, provided there is no attempt to play at Foot Ball in the public streets or thoroughfares, and these Sports, with such others as may be found desirable and proper, will be the basis of those of future years ; but should there be any such attempt to play at Foot Ball in any public street or thoroughfare, the other Sports will be immediately discontinued and never afterwards renewed, and the Subscriptions (after deducting expenses) will be returned, so that any persons who may encourage a breach of the law will not only be the enemies of those they may lead to punishment, and render necessary stronger measures to prevent the recurrence of the Foot Ball another year, but will be open to the reproach of having prevented the Sports contemplated for the present and future years.—

THE HOLMES,

Shrove Tuesday, Feb. 4,

AT TWO O'CLOCK PRECISELY.

FOR MEN.

Grand Pedestrian Hurdle Race.

First Prize, £1.—Second, 10s.—Third, 5s.

Jumping Match for height,

WITH A POLE.—Prize, 5s.

FOOT RACE.

First Prize, 10s.—Second, 5s.—Third, 2s. 6d.

Jumping Match for height,

WITHOUT A POLE.—Prize, 5s.

Foot Race, blindfolded, straight.

First Prize, 7s. 6d.—Second, 5s.—Third, 2s. 6d.

Jumping Match for length,

WITH A POLE.—Three Trials.—Prize, 5s.

BAG RACE.

EACH COMPETITOR TO BRING A BAG FOR HIMSELF.
First Prize, 7s. 6d.—Second, 5s.—Third, 2s. 6d.

Jumping Match for length,

WITHOUT A POLE.—Three Trials.—Prize, 5s.

Handicap Race for Men carrying Boys.

First Prize, 5s.—Second, 3s.—Third, 2s.

The greatest distance at 20 hops

Prize, 5s.

Wheelbarrow Race, blindfolded.

Each competitor to bring a Wheelbarrow for himself.—Prize 5s.

Hop, Step and Jump.

Prize, 5s.

Grinning Match through collars

Each competitor to bring a collar for himself.
Prize, 2s. 6d.

Ash Wednesday, Feb. 5,

AT TWO O'CLOCK PRECISELY,

FOR BOYS.

The same Sports, with similar Prizes at half the amounts as those on Shrove-Tuesday (for Men) excepting the Handicap Race and Grinning Match, for which the following will be substituted :—

Plum Pudding & Treacle Match.

First Prize, 2s. 6d.—Second, 1s. 6d.—Third, 1s.

Swarming a Pole.

Prize, a New Hat and 2s. 6d.

As there may be some who prefer to the above Sports, **FOOT BALL** where no public or private injury can arise, there will (in addition to the above Prizes) be on **SHROVE TUESDAY** for MEN, **TEN POUNDS**; and on **ASH WEDNESDAY**, for BOYS, **FIVE POUNDS**, given to the **FOOT BALL PLAYERS** for their own Game, on their not playing in the Holmes, or in any public street or thoroughfare.

The other Sports will be under the direction of Managers, who will decide as to the number, ages and qualifications of Competitors, distances and other questions ; and the Entrance of Names for each Prize will take place on each day, at the COMMITTEE ROOM, COCKPIT HILL, until half-past One o'clock.—Preference will be given to those who enter first ; but should the Entry not be full, other Competitors will be allowed to enter up to the time of starting.

It is amongst the objects of these Sports to promote a social and kindly feeling in all who partake in them, and to give a fair field for manly exercises and innocent recreation, free from all immorality and vicious excitement, and the assistance of every well-disposed person who may be present is relied upon in carrying out these intentions.—No one will be allowed to sell liquor in the Holmes, or in any boat on the River or Canal adjoining. A blanket will be ready on the Ground, and any Person who offends, by quarrelling or improper conduct, will contribute his share to the amusements by being tossed in it.

That all may have an equal chance of seeing the Sports, it is hoped the directions of the persons who may be appointed to keep the Ground will be complied with in a spirit of good humour. No horsemen allowed on the Ground.

Bands of Music will attend, and if from a heavy fall of rain or snow the Sports should be prevented on the days proposed, the Public may rely on their taking place on subsequent days, as early as possible, when the weather will permit.

There will be a **TEA FESTIVAL** at the Mechanics' Hall, Wardwick, on Wednesday evening, which will be concluded with dancing and other

104 L.G.Wright born in Derby, played for Derbyshire and England in 1885.

105 Sir Francis Ley who gave the Baseball Ground to Derby County Football Club.

103 *(left)* Poster advertising the sports organised by the town council as a rival attraction for the Shrovetide Football Match.

who made 1,000 runs in the 1895 season. In 1900 the club signed its first West Indian cricketer, Charles Olivierre. Notable successes in the 20th century have included winning the county championship in 1936 and the Natwest Trophy in 1981.

The Derby County Football Club, or the Rams as they are known, started in 1884 as a means to keep the county cricketers fit during the winter. By that date a half-day holiday on Saturday was normal for most workers, and with a pool of people wanting something to do on a Saturday afternoon there was always a good audience for the county football club's matches. At this point someone realised that if a special ground were reserved for the matches an admission fee could be charged and a profit made. The first ground was next to the cricket ground in Nottingham Road. It was paid for by a group of shareholders who must have had severe doubts as to whether they would actually make any money from the enterprise as the club ended up firmly at the bottom of the newly formed Football League in 1884, and had to apply for re-election. After that it began to improve.

In 1895 the club moved to a ground beside the Vulcan Foundry in Litchurch, owned by Sir Francis Ley. On a visit to America Sir Francis had seen and become entranced by baseball. On his return he founded a successful baseball club which played on the ground beside his works. When he lost interest in baseball he gave the ground to the football club, which has played on the Baseball Ground ever since.

The Derby County Football Club takes its nickname the 'Rams' from the folk song *The Derby Ram*. The actual origin of this song is unknown. It first appears in print in 1833. It describes a gigantic ram with miraculous attributes. These sample verses come from one of the many versions of the song:

> As I was going to Derby,
> All on a market day,
> I met the finest ram, Sir
> That ever was fed on hay.
>
> The wool upon his back, Sir
> Reach'd up to the sky
> The eagles built their nests there,
> For I heard the young ones cry,
>
> The space between the horns, Sir
> Was far as man could reach,
> And there they built a pulpit
> But no one in it preach'd

106   The Derby Ram, a sandstone sculpture commissioned by the city council in 1995. It stands at the junction of Albion and East Streets.

> The butcher that killed this ram, Sir
> Was drowned in the blood,
> And all the people of Derby
> Were carried away in the flood

and so on through all the parts of the ram's anatomy.

Antiquarians suggest that the Derby Ram harks back to Norse sagas and the old tup of *Edda's* saga who turned out to be the Giant *Ymir*. Others relate it to the ram taken around with the mummers performing the Christmas play.

Other entertainments that were popular in 19th-century Derby included freak shows such as an exhibition of the midget Tom Thumb and the circus. In the 1870s there was even a permanent circus in Derby, Keith's Circus in Princes Street, which was unfortunately burnt down in 1879 with great loss of livestock. Family concerts were another form of entertainment. These were held in the Corn Exchange and 'Mendelssohn-like' oratorios were performed by amateurs. For the more rumbustious there were music halls. The first such venture was the Star Music Hall which opened in Princes Street in 1873. The Palace of Varieties opened in 1897. This was reputed to be a very rough place with at least one fight an evening.

Those who wanted a more sedate evening out could go to the theatre. In 1885 the Grand Theatre opened in Babington Lane, but was closed by fire almost immediately. It re-opened a year later to provide good quality entertainment with top London actors such as Sir Frank Benson playing the lead.

Two types of production stand out as being especially popular at the Grand, and were probably attended by all who could afford it. The first of these was the pantomime. Unlike today there was a choice of pantomimes across the Christmas season performed by different touring companies. For example, in December 1895 'Aladdin' was performed, followed by 'Dick Whittington' and 'Sindbad the Sailor' in January 1896. The popularity of these performances can be judged by the fact that seat prices went up in the pantomime season, but the theatre was still sold out.

The other show which was incredibly popular was a play called *The Sign of the Cross*. This is recorded

107   The Grand Theatre in Babington Lane.

as pulling in capacity audiences wherever it was performed. Such was its popularity in Derby that it was performed several times a year by different touring companies, and the railways ran special late trains for theatre goers from Burton, Tamworth, Nottingham and Chesterfield, and all stations in between.

Why was the play so popular? It was a tale of early Christians in Nero's Rome. But it was not its morally uplifting overtones of Christian fortitude that people went to see, but the fact that it included a Roman orgy scene with scantily clad girls in it. In the early 20th century the live theatre was to be threatened by the cinema, which would eventually bare more flesh than the Victorians would have thought possible.

Chapter Ten

Health, Housing, Poverty and the Co-operative Movement—Derby in the Late 19th Century

———◆———

In 1841 the population of Derby was 32,741. This rose steadily during the last half of the 19th century to 69,266 in 1901. Many of the town's working-class population lived in overcrowded and insanitary conditions consisting of badly built terraced houses or noisome enclosed courts. Few houses had access to piped water and the streets were running with sewage from cess pits and middens interlaced with offal from slaughter houses thrown out onto the common highway. Such were the conditions in the town observed by the Commission into the State of Large Towns in 1844.

It reports that, although the national average death rate stood at 22 per 1,000, at this time in Derby it was 28 per 1,000. The Commissioners attributed this to the lack of drains and sewers in the town. The report said that: 'Derby, with serious structural defects as respect of streets is almost unequalled in its neglect of drainage and sewage. It is also very deficient in water for domestic purposes and for cleaning. The sickness and mortality are great in the districts inhabited by the working classes.'

In these districts severe overcrowding was found; people were crammed into courts erected as infill between existing houses. The courts lacked ventilation and the basic requirements of sanitation. Especially bad were the areas around Bridge Street at the back of Friargate and the courts off Sadlergate. Housing adjoining Burton Road and Eagle Street was also singled out as being in deplorable condition.

Shortly before the publication of the report the Markeaton Brook had inundated low-lying areas of the town. Inspection of the damage this had caused revealed to the shocked authorities naked children frolicking in the polluted waters. Dr. William Barker, a member of the Derby Sanitary

Committee, reported to the Commission into the Sanitary Conditions of the Labouring Population in 1842 that Willow Row was probably the worst street in the town. Willow Row was again singled out in 1848 by Edward Cressy, Derby's Public Health Inspector, who described finding 102 people sharing two privies in the row.

The Commission of Inquiry into the State of Large Towns decided that the root of the problem in Derby lay in the fact that the antiquated Improvement Commission still had responsibility for draining the town and cleaning the streets. The Improvement Commission surrendered its powers to the council in 1848, and a year later a new water works was opened to provide the town with a relatively clean water supply. A new sewage system which came into use in the 1860s managed to lower the death rate to 18 per 1,000.[1]

Street improvements continued in Derby throughout the late 19th century. In the 1850s Thomas Roe, one of the town's mayors, pioneered the widening of St James Street and improved Sadlergate and Siddals Road. The open brook at the junction of Sadlergate and Bold Lane was covered over and a good roadway called The Strand constructed. Irongate was also widened. Traffic confusion was sorted out by the construction of Exeter bridge. The removal of Rotten Row created a larger market place, and the elegant new Market Hall was opened in 1865. In the same year the Piazza buildings on the Market Place, which had become decayed and insanitary, were demolished as was the *Dusty Miller* public house in Tennant Street, which also added to space in the market.

Despite efforts to improve them, in 1870 the Walker Lane, Willow Row and Bold Lane areas were

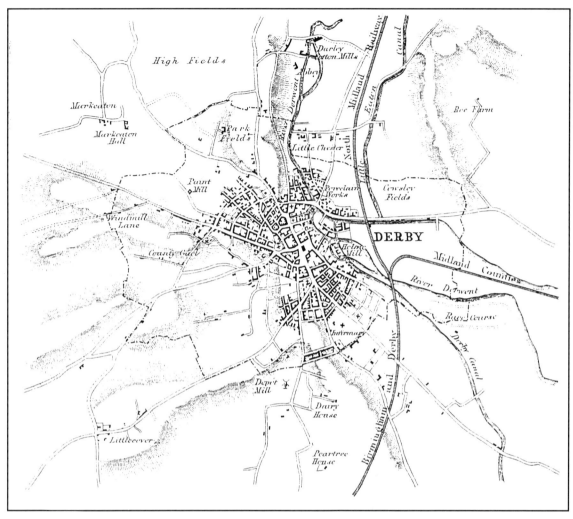

108 Map of Derby produced to accompany Edward Cresy's 1849 report. Note that the town was still surrounded by open fields at that date.

still overcrowded slums in which 555 dwellings housed a population of 2,503 persons. Under the Artisans Dwelling Act it became possible for the council to borrow money to rebuild slum areas. Henry Bemrose, who was mayor in 1877 of an enlarged borough which now included Litchurch and part of Normanton, suggested that this should be done but there was considerable opposition to this from property owners and ratepayers. The council persisted and work went ahead demolishing houses considered unfit for human habitation in the area, and widening Walker Lane and Willow Row. At the same time Bag Lane, St Peter's and East Street were widened and the slums on the north side of

Bag Lane were demolished. These were positive efforts to improve the conditions of the working class.[2]

Edwin Chadwick who was one of the authors of the report of the inquiry into the sanitary conditions of the working class was also responsible for the report on the working of the Old Poor Law. Public opinion had forced the government to act on the Poor Law. The Poor Rate which householders with property worth over ten pounds a year paid had reached astronomical proportions and it was felt that the system was being abused, with too many paupers being relieved outside the workhouse.

109 In 1880 William Wiggington wrote a treatise on model dwellings for the working classes which used Derby as a case study.

The Poor Law Amendment Act of 1834 recommended that relief for all able-bodied paupers was to cease unless they entered a workhouse which was to be built and maintained by a union of parishes. Each of Derby's parishes already had a workhouse. These were inspected by the Poor Law Commissioners. They commended St Werburgh's workhouse. It applied the workhouse rules and would give no outdoor relief. As a result it had the lowest poor rate of the borough. The commissioners attributed this success to Henry Mosley the printer who lived in The Friary, who had made use of the Select Vestry Act to set the Poor Rate at a low level. St Alkmund's workhouse was also praised for its efficiency which was due mainly to the influence of William Strutt of St Helen's House. All Saints' and St Peter's had high poor rates of 2s. 6d. in the pound, but St Michael's, where the poor rate was 3s. 4d., was condemned for pampering its paupers who were earning wages as well as receiving poor relief.

It was decided that as a start the new Derby Union Workhouse would be based on St Werburgh's workhouse in Walker Lane. The other workhouses were to be sold off and eventually a new purpose-built workhouse would be constructed from the proceeds. Although acquiescing to the demands of the new Poor Law, outdoor relief continued in Derby. John Columbell was appointed relieving officer. Most of his work was spent in relieving aged

and infirm paupers too frail to move, and in disbursing money for coffins. He also had charge of paying for those in special education such as William Holmes, aged 11, who was at the Blind Asylum in Edgbaston. The numbers of those asking for outdoor relief rose in the late 1830s and '40s. Columbell reported that many in the town earned no more than 5s. a week and could not support themselves.

The Act of Settlement of 1660, which made poor relief available only in the parish of legal settlement, was still being invoked in Derby in the late 1830s. Requests were made for money to help paupers with settlement entitlement from as far afield as Salford by Manchester, Amersham, Buckinghamshire and one young pauper boy, Thomas Axon, was returned to Bedford by boat.

The new workhouse was built in Osmaston Road. Although it had stringent rules and families were split up, compared with other similar institutions Derby workhouse had a humanitarian attitude to its unfortunate inmates.

It was administered by a governor and matron, and a schoolmaster and mistress to teach the children. The first governor and matron, Ratcliffe Gawthorne and his wife Ann, were dismissed for inefficiency and were replaced by Mr. and Mrs. William Webster. The Websters reorganised the workhouse, putting all the mentally disturbed inmates together and setting up a nursery for the babies. Young children were allowed to sleep with their parents, and in the daytime the pauper babies rocked peacefully, six to a wicker cradle. Sometimes older children were taken out of the workhouse to play and to fly kites. This must have been a welcome release from their usual day which started at 6 o'clock and was devoted throughout to lessons and work until they went to bed in the early evening.

In 1877 the workhouse moved again, to Uttoxeter Road. The Workhouse Commissioners also administered the City Hospital which was built on the opposite side of the road to the workhouse in 1914. The workhouse survived as a geriatric hospital until 1988 when it was demolished. In 1884 Derbyshire Children's Hospital was opened in North Street, built partly through the generosity of Michael Bass the borough M.P. and Sir Abraham Woodiwiss, the mayor at that time. Sir Abraham, who was born at Duffield but moved to The Pastures in Littleover in 1866, was a partner in a firm of railway contractors.

The Rowditch Asylum, now known as the Kingsway Hospital, was opened in 1888 with Dr. Macphail as its first medical superintendent. A hospital for women and a contagious diseases hospital completed the provision for health in the 19th century.[3]

The 1870 Education Act, which made education compulsory for all children between five and 10 years, meant changes in the education system in Derby. Prior to this children had been educated at church or ragged schools. When the newly elected School Board met in 1871 it decided to make up the deficiency of places for scholars by leasing premises in Ashbourne Road and Kedleston Street and to build a new school in Gerard Street. An attendance officer was appointed with a salary of £80 a year and free board and lodgings at the School Board's offices in Friargate. The truancy officer had a uniform of a blue frock coat, waterproof cap and two pairs of trousers. The frock coat was embroidered in red with the words 'School Board Officer'. Not only did his commanding figure put fear into the truants and their parents but their names and the fines their parents had to pay for the truancy appeared in the local papers so that everyone knew about their disgraceful behaviour. Constant truants were sent to the Old Lock up in the Cornmarket as a warning. If they still persisted in truanting they were sentenced for a spell in a Reformatory or a School of Industry.

The School Board soon erected new buildings in Abbey and Traffic Streets and Ashbourne and St

110   A lesson in progress in a 19th-century educational establishment in Derby.

James Roads, and in 1888 the first school to provide secondary education for those who required it opened in Gerard Street. The emphasis at the Gerard Street school was on the practical. Girls were taught cookery and home economics, whilst boys learnt practical science, building construction and maths.

A Diocesan Institute for Training School-mistresses was founded by Bishop Lonsdale of Lichfield in 1850. Housed in a handsome red-brick building in Uttoxeter New Road, the college was to become Bishop Lonsdale's Training College before being incorporated into the Derbyshire College of Higher Education, which formed the nucleus of the University of Derby. Other components of the University of Derby were the College of Art and the Technical College which merged in 1876 and were housed in a red-brick gothic style building in Green Lane. Further teacher training was supplied by the Derby Pupil Teachers Centre which opened in 1889 with William Creswell as its principal. Thus it can be seen that the town has a long commitment to higher education.[4]

Derby was rightly proud of its mayors in the 19th century. Many were distinguished industrialists and professional men who carried out their work with great enthusiasm. Notable amongst them were the Strutt family who originated from Blackwell in Derbyshire, where the founder of the family Jedediah Strutt was born in 1726. Jedediah was apprenticed to Ralph Massey, a wheelwright of Findern, and after his apprenticeship spent a spell as a farmer before turning his attention to the hosiery industry. In 1758 he took out a patent on a stocking frame which produced a rib known as the 'Derby Rib'. Ten years later Jedediah went into textile production as a partner of Richard Arkwright with mills at Cromford and Belper. This partnership was dissolved in 1782 and the Strutt name became synonymous with Belper and its mills.

Jedediah Strutt ended his days at Exeter House in 1797. He left three sons, William, George and Joseph. William and Joseph were to be intimately connected with Derby. William, born in 1756, shared his father's interest in mechanics and developed a patent system for warming and ventilating buildings which he used in his design for the Derby Royal Infirmary. William, who was a friend of Erasmus Darwin and Robert Owen, married Barbara Evans, the daughter of Thomas

111 Bishop Lonsdale's Diocesan Training College in Uttoxeter New Road.

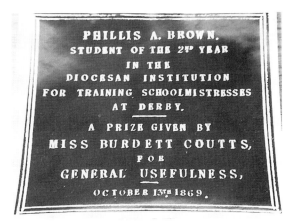

112 Prize certificate issued to a student teacher.

113 Jedediah Strutt 1726-97. Founder of the Strutt family mill owners and benefactors in Derby and its surroundings.

Evans of Allestree Hall. They lived in St Helen's House.

Joseph Strutt was born in 1766. It was he who generously gave the town the Arboretum, and his work for the town included serving as the first mayor of Derby after the Municipal Corporations Act of 1835. He promoted the Mechanics Institute and the Lancastrian School and was a personal friend of Joseph Lancaster. He amassed a large collection of books and pictures, and such was his generosity that anyone who was interested was invited into his house in St Peter's Street to view them. He died there in 1844.

114   Joseph Strutt, 1766-1844. Donated the Arboretum to the town, and sponsored the Lancastrian School.

William's son Edward was born in 1801 at St Helen's House. Educated at Cambridge, Edward broke away from his industrial background and entered the law. He was a friend of Jeremy Bentham the philosopher of utilitarianism and John Stuart Mill. He entered Parliament in 1830 as Liberal MP for the borough and kept the seat until 1847, when

bribery allegations against his agent led him to be disqualified from sitting. Later he was to re-enter Parliament as MP for Arundel in 1851. He was created Baron Belper in 1856.[5]

Edward Strutt's place in Parliament was taken by another Liberal, Michael Thomas Bass. Born in 1799, Bass was a member of the great Burton brewing family. His early association with the town came from his activities with the Derbyshire Yeomanry, and he was part of the company that helped to control the Reform Bill Riots in 1832. He was an active Member of Parliament, instrumental in getting a private members bill through Parliament, which allowed householders to take out injunctions to ban street musicians from their vicinity. He campaigned with the railway workers in 1870 for a cut in their working hours and helped to found the Railway Servants Orphanage in Derby. He gave the town the recreation ground which still bears his name. This was opened in 1867 with peals of church bells, flags and bunting and a procession followed by sports and games. He also gave the town the buildings to house its free library and art museum, the foundation stone for which was laid by Bass in 1871.

Despite such displays of civic confidence, Derby was subject to economic recession and hardship for many of its working folk in the late 19th century. A bad winter in 1885 precipitated much distress, and in 1906 another bad winter and chronic unemployment made it necessary to set up a special fund to help the poor and needy.

The hungry years of the 1840s with high prices and much unemployment led a group of 'pioneers' in Rochdale to join together to form a co-operative society for buying produce wholesale and selling to its members who received a dividend of the profits. In 1849 Jonathan Henderson, the secretary of the Carpenters and Joiners Society in Derby, wrote to the Rochdale Pioneers for information about their society, and as a result 12 carpenters and joiners with a capital of £2 started the Derby Co-operative Society in a yard off Sadlergate. With their £2 investment they purchased a pair of second-hand scales and some flour from Shaw the miller in St Michael's Lane. They were in business, selling flour to their members on three evenings a week from 8-10 p.m. Each member of the society served in the store in turn, whilst Thomas Rushton Brown was the shopman in charge of provisions. When in 1857 the society moved to two rooms in Victoria Street, its sales averaged £10 a week. Until this date the society had been confined to members of the Carpenters' and Joiners' Union, but in 1859 the decision was taken to offer the general public a chance to join the society. In the same year the society moved again to a hay loft at 47 Full Street, known as Penny Bank Yard. A year later the society had 40 members. They broadcast the benefits of belonging to the society so well that soon prospective members were flocking to join the society, as many as 36 being enrolled in one evening. A further

115 The Free Library, now Derby Central Library, given to the town by Michael Bass.

promotion exercise involved the distribution of leaflets to 4,000 houses, and having the Derby Co-Operative Society painted in large letters on their shop front in Penny Bank Yard.

By 1861 the society was providing social and educational events for its members, and branches were opened in Park Street and Nun Street, where the first society bakery was situated. In 1865 the idea of a new central store was mooted, and in 1868 the Society purchased a small parcel of land in Albert Street and appointed the firm of architects Thomson and Young to design a purpose-built store for them. This opened in 1871.

At the end of the 19th century there was a network of co-operative society shops across Derby and in 1899 the membership stood at 13,179 and profits at £42,444. As well as paying dividends to members, the society extended its business interests. A building loan department was opened in 1876, and the society itself went into the construction industry—Industrial, Co-Operative and Provident Streets in Normanton being co-operative society developments. A model dairy was opened at Spondon in 1908, and a small farm purchased on Nottingham Road.[6]

The early development of the society could not have taken place without the dedication of its organisers. These included women, as the Co-Operative Society had radical views on equal employment for women. In 1859 the minutes of the A.G.M. show women registering proposals for discussion, and women were employed beside men on the shop floor. Robert Hilliard, the society's president, actively promoted women's interests in a speech he made to the 1879 A.G.M. 'Women must lead in this co-operative movement,' he said, 'for co-operation is essentially a woman's question ...' The society encouraged women to become active in politics and in 1919 Mrs. Jessie Unsworth, secretary of the Women's Guild, became the first candidate of the Co-Operative Political Council in Derby to stand for election in local government.

Women in general began to play a more important rôle in public affairs. They were permitted to act as Poor Law Guardians and as members of School Boards. They also published books and pamphlets which show that middle-class women took an especial interest in the education of girls. Mrs. Corden Roe, wife of Thomas Roe, Derby's mayor in 1863, published a pamphlet on this topic, and also wrote two history textbooks for use in schools. She was a noted lecturer and public speaker much in demand around the town.

Other women, such as Mrs. Duesbury, concerned themselves with the temperance movement which had a strong following in the

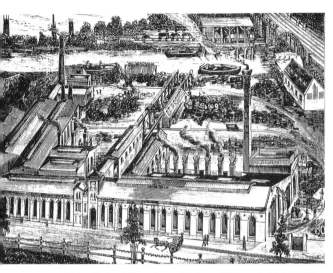

116   Haslam's Foundry at the time of the royal visit in 1891.

117   Sir Alfred Haslam at the time of his knighthood, 1891.

town. The temperance movement precipitated a disturbance in November 1871 when it asked Sir Charles Dilkes to speak at the Temperance Hall. This coincided with the introduction of by-laws that curbed the number of hours in a day during which alcohol could be sold. An 'organised' attempt was made to stop Sir Charles speaking, which resulted in a series of fights during which the Temperance Hall was wrecked and those on the platform forced to flee. Numerous arrests followed this fracas.

An enlightened and innovative employer in the town was Sir Alfred Haslam whose Union Foundry and Engineering Works was one of the most prestigious foundries in the country. Sir Alfred came from a Derby family connected with the iron trade. He was educated in the town and served an apprenticeship with the Midland Railway Company before moving on to work at Sir William Armstrong's company on Tyneside. He moved back to Derby in 1868.[7]

Sir Alfred's main claim to fame is the invention and manufacture of the Haslam Refrigerator which was used on board warships, liners and most notably on cargo ships bringing meat from Australia, New Zealand and South America. The first shipment of meat carried in a refrigerated cargo sheep arrived in this country from New Zealand in 1882. Frozen imported meat was cheaper than home produced meat, which meant that the working class could afford to have meat more frequently. It is probably to Sir Alfred Haslam's invention that we owe the tradition of the Sunday roast.

Close to his works in Little Chester Sir Alfred built well appointed houses for his workforce which can be distinguished by a diamond shaped lozenge of bricks on the upper storey. On the opposite side of the road to the factory he built a semi-circular canteen and rest room for the workers. He also financed enlargements to St Paul's Church in Chester Green, which had been dedicated in 1850 with free seating for 600 parishioners.

It was during Sir Alfred's mayoral year in 1891 that Queen Victoria paid a state visit to the town, travelling by train to be met at the Midland Station by a thousand spectators lining the platform. Her Majesty, accompanied by her daughter Princess Beatrice of Battenburg and family, was helped from the train by her Scots and Indian servants. She proceeded to the Market Place for an official welcome and then to the infirmary where Alfred Haslam, resplendent in a court suit of black silk, three-cornered hat of black velvet and a robe of crimson Genoa velvet, was knighted. To commemorate his day of triumph Sir Alfred gave the town a statue of Queen Victoria to stand at The Spot on the junction of London and Osmaston Roads. This was unveiled by Edward VII in 1906. Sir Alfred was later to serve as the Unionist MP for the borough.[8]

Public transport in the town also developed in the late 19th century into a comprehensive network. Wallace Wallis's fleet of horsebuses connected the station with the market place from

118 A horse bus in the Market Place at the end of the 19th century.

119 A map produced by William Bemrose and Sons in 1895. This copy was used for sanitation purposes; each circle represents a trough closet.

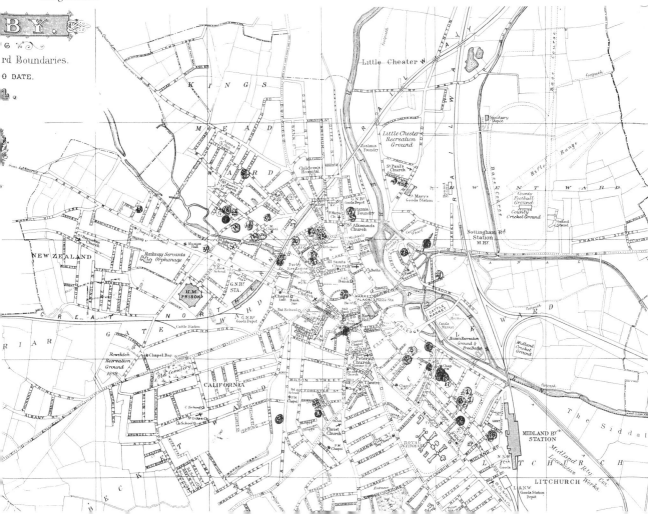

the 1840s onwards. In 1880 a horse-drawn tramway was added to connect the Midland and Great Northern stations. After the company which ran this went bankrupt, the corporation purchased it and decided to abandon the antiquated horse-drawn system and to electrify it. Work on this was completed by 1904 and it ran until 1933 when it was replaced by a trolley-bus system. A public bus service linked Derby with other villages and towns, and in 1913 the Trent Bus Company began a regular bus service between Derby and Ashbourne followed by services to Alfreton, Burton on Trent, Chesterfield and Melbourne.

Electric lighting was turned on in the centre of Derby in 1891. Ten lamps specially prepared for the occasion illuminated the Market Place and Cornmarket. The whole of the central area had electric street lamps by 1909.

The rapid increase in population meant that the old churchyards became overcrowded with no room for any more burials. To accommodate the town's dead a large municipal cemetery was opened on Nottingham Road in 1855. In 1890 this too was filling up and it was proposed that the free fourth-class graves known as the Poor Man's Ground should be re-opened to put in more burials, unless friends and relatives of those already buried were willing to purchase the plot. An observer described this area of the cemetery as being marked by little iron crosses or lathes tacked or tied together by string and flowers placed in cordial bottles and jam jars. Little children were buried in squares of four and often the grave was marked by a favourite plaything of the child such as a seashell, or perhaps a little china ornament. The same observer remarked on the long rows of babies' graves often marked only by the mound. The innocent sleepers beneath the mounds now lie within the sound of the roar of incessant traffic from Nottingham Road and the A52, contemporary evidence of Derby's long affair with the combustion engine which was to start in the early years of the 20th century.[9]

Chapter Eleven

Rolls-Royce and War—
Derby in the Early 20th Century

The 20th century opened in Derby with the return of the 4th Derbyshire Militia from the Boer War. The militia had acquitted itself bravely in the war, losing 36 men; it was given a heroes' welcome by the town. Arriving at Pear Tree station, the men marched to the market place to be welcomed by the mayor. This was followed by a banquet at the *Royal Hotel.*

In 1901 the population of the town was 69,266; this rose dramatically to 123,410 in 1911. The rise was the result of the extension of the borough boundaries in 1901 to include parts of Alvaston, Chaddesden, Osmaston by Derby and Spondon. A proposal to include Darley Abbey and Littleover was deleted from the bill to extend the boundaries by the Parliamentary Committee discussing it. This was due to strong local opposition by the occupants of these villages who wished to maintain their own identity. The 1911 census shows that there were 27,405 inhabited houses in the borough with 1,406 standing empty. On average 4.5 people lived in each house, which equates to the modern nuclear family of parents and 2.5 children. In 1914 there were 1,031 marriages registered in the town, 3,011 births and 1,637 deaths with a death rate of 13 per 1,000, which shows an improvement on the 19th-century figure.

In the 1901 bill the town was divided into 16 wards instead of eight as previously; each ward returned three councillors to the town council. The composition of the council was 48 elected councillors and 16 aldermen. Between them they had responsibility for education in the borough, as well as maintaining the streets and sewage in good order, and providing recreational facilities and a library service. The town council also provided garden allotments in built-up areas such as Ashbourne and Mansfield Roads, and at the Rowditch. In all 45 acres of land in the town was given over to 655 allotment plots.[1]

The town council ran an electric tramway in the town. Early routes went along Babington Lane and Burton Road. In 1904 the service was extended to include a circular route through New Normanton and Pear Tree, whilst in 1906-7 trams were routed along Ashbourne, Nottingham, and Uttoxeter Roads. Other services that the council provided included the fire brigade, which in 1916 consisted of 11 firemen and one motor engine as well as other appliances. A network of 23 fire alarm boxes was placed across the town on factories such as Bemrose & Sons printing works in Park Street, public houses like the *Babington Arms* in Burton Road and on public buildings such as the police station, in order to alert townspeople and firemen of a conflagration. In the same year the borough police force had a strength of 153 men.

The mayor and council played an important rôle in the visit of Edward VII to the town in 1906 when he unveiled the statue of Queen Victoria given to the town by a former mayor, Sir Alfred Haslam. Originally this stood at The Spot, but it is now in the grounds of the Derbyshire Royal Infirmary. A few weeks after the king's visit the mayor who had greeted him, Edwin Ann, was given a knighthood. Edwin Ann was born in Swansea in 1852 and had come to Derby in 1882 to open a drapery in St Peter's Street. This developed into the Midland Drapery Company with a branch in East Street, Derby as well as other towns in the Midlands employing upwards of three hundred shop assistants. A paternalistic employer, Ann is recorded as taking

120   1906 royal visit; a wet day in Derby.

his workers on excursions to Chatsworth and other places of interest.

Another mayor in the first decade of the 20th century was William Blews Robotham, a solicitor noted for his work with the temperance movement. He preached on temperance at the Brewster Sessions, where landlords of public houses applied for licences to sell liqueur, and during his mayoralty in 1909

the town was host to the National British Women's Temperance Association. The events included a tee-total reception in the Drill Hall with entertainment supplied by the Derby Pupil Teacher Centre's Ladies Choir. William Robotham was also active in the work of the National Society for the Prevention of Cruelty to Children and the National Lifeboat Institution. On Saturday, 17 July 1909 he organised

121   The New Infirmary buildings, opened by Edward VII on his visit to the town in 1906.

122   Procession of a lifeboat through the town in 1909, sponsored by William Robotham.

a gala in aid of the lifeboats which included a procession from the town centre to Darley Abbey Park, where the old Worthing lifeboat crewed by the Grimsby lifeboat men was launched onto the Derwent, bearing the mayor and alderman Robert Chambers.[2]

In 1903 Herbert Spencer, a famous son of Derby, died. Spencer has been described as the founder of sociology. He was born in 1820 in Exeter Row close to the market place in Derby and was educated in Derby, but also spent some time with his uncle in Bath. At the age of 17 he became an assistant schoolmaster in Derby. Bored with this, he left to become an engineer with the Birmingham and Gloucester Railway Company which he hated, but whilst working with the railway company his ideas became increasingly radical. He became a prolific correspondent to the newspapers and to radical journals such as *The Non-Conformist*. In 1843 he produced a report on the drainage of Derby suggesting improvements that would prevent the frequent flooding of the town. When he was sacked by the railway company, he entered journalism full time by taking up the editorship of *The Pilot*. In 1866 he moved to London to become sub-editor

on *The Economist*. All this time he was working on a system of ideas which he called 'synthetic philosophy'; this encompassed a number of disciplines including ethics, psychology, metaphysics and biology. In 1862 he published a book called *First Principles*, which outlined his ideas—the first book on sociology to be published. It was followed by *A Study of Sociology* in 1873 and *Descriptive Sociology* in 1881. He died in Brighton and his ashes were scattered in Highgate Cemetery. The bulk of his estate was put into trust to carry on his work on descriptive sociology. A Spencerian Society was formed in Derby with the aim of 'drawing together those who were desirous of studying philosophy and other subjects.'

Other societies and institutes dedicated to study and debate in the town included the Mechanics Institute and the Derby Society for the Extension of University Teaching, which gave lectures for an annual fee of 10s. The Midland Railway (Derby) Literary and Debating Society, in 1913 had the object of illustrating and discussing the general workings of railways and other means of transport and subjects of a literary nature. The Midland Railway company also had a natural history society

123   Green Lane in the early 20th century.

By far the most popular type of entertainment in the early years of the 20th century was the cinema: by 1916 Derby had five cinemas. The Cosy Picture House in London Road had continuous performances. This cinema's attractions included the snug boxes for two which could be hired for the price of 2s. The Picture House in Babington Lane was part of the Midland Theatre chain. It boasted a café, lounge and orchestra. The White Hall also had a café. The Spot Theatre in London Road claimed that it showed a 'continuous exhibition of the Latest Pictures in Black and White, only the latest masterpieces exhibited'. The prices of seats in the cinemas ranged from 3d. to 6d., whilst the Cosy Picture House had half-price tickets for children and ran a matinée for children at 2.30 on a Saturday afternoon.[3]

In 1900 the town got its first Labour MP— Richard Bell was returned as one of the borough members with Sir Thomas Roe, a Liberal, as the other. They were re-elected in the 1906 election. During an acrimonious campaign Joseph Chamberlain, the radical Liberal from Birmingham, attempted to address a meeting in the town, but was prevented from doing so by rowdyism and overcrowding in the hall. In 1910 Sir Thomas was again returned, this time in the company of James 'Jimmy' Thomas, a prominent member of the Association of Railworkers.

Perhaps the most important event for the town in the first decade of the 20th century was the arrival of Rolls-Royce. The early history of the firm takes place away from Derby. F. H. Royce, the engineering brains of the firm, was born in 1863 in a village close to Peterborough. The youngest son of a large family, he left school at the age of 14 and became a newsboy in London for W. H. Smith. Later he returned to Peterborough to take up an apprenticeship with the Great Northern Railway, but due to financial hardship was forced to give this up and take employment in Leeds as a machine tool operative earning 11s. a week. From Leeds he returned to London to work with the Electric Light and Power Company, but shortly after he was appointed chief electrician to the Liverpool branch of this company it went bankrupt and Royce was unemployed. Undismayed he entered into a partnership with another redundant employee of the company and started a firm in Manchester which

and a chess club, whilst athletics and rowing clubs catered for those with more active interests. Both commercial and amateur football remained popular in the town. As well as the 'Rams' there were amateur leagues, such as the Wednesday Football League, and the Amateur Football League, that organised competitions. Cricket was also popular, as were fishing, golf, hockey, swimming and tennis, whilst the council ran its own roller-skating rink. This opened in 1907 in the converted Reginald Street baths. Here for the price of 6d., which included skate hire, the enthusiast could skate on a purpose-built maple wood floor.

The Grand Theatre continued to offer twice-nightly entertainment, whilst the Hippodrome on the corner of Green Lane and Macklin Street described itself as a variety theatre for all the family, with the most up-to-date turns appearing twice nightly. The Coliseum music hall opposite to the General Post Office also showed variety turns, and in the summer a high-class concert party performed in Normanton Gardens.

made electrical appliances such as electric bells and fuses. Soon electric switchboards and dynamos were added to the firm's products, and it was with the latter that the firm made its mark. Such was its success that in 1893 Royce had sufficient capital to enable him to import a Deauville car from France.

He purchased the motor from France because of a lack of a satisfactory British alternative. Royce was well aware that there was a gap in the market that needed filling, and the first thing he did on receiving the car was to take it to pieces to see how it was made. He found what he thought to be a good design marred by some careless workmanship, and he was convinced that he could produce a better model. He set about doing this, starting with a two-cylinder ten-horsepower car, followed by 15-, 20- and 30-hp prototype cars, which all received great acclaim from the national press.

One of those who recognised the quality of Royce's work was a flying enthusiast, the Honourable Charles Rolls. In 1904 he contacted Royce with a proposition in which he became the sole agent for selling Royce's cars from his London showroom. He also demonstrated the car's paces in touring car races. In 1905, at the end of the first year of their partnership, there was a full order book for the cars. A year later the partnership of Rolls-Royce was officially registered at Company House.

It was obvious by this time that the company had outgrown the Manchester workshop. A public share issue was floated on the Stock Exchange, and with the money raised from this, and with the help of a wealthy Yorkshire industrialist A.H. Briggs, the company started to look for new premises.

It had already built up a skilled and loyal workforce so its first choice was for new premises in Manchester. But Manchester was far removed from the showrooms in London. Eventually there was a short list of four sites: Stretford in Manchester, Coventry and Leicester in the Midlands, and land already owned by A.H. Briggs in Bradford.

The firm was looking for the availability of raw materials to make the cars, and easy access to the London market. Derby felt that it could supply these needs and the town council, through the agency of the Derby Development Committee, put together a package to offer to Rolls-Royce. They offered a cheap, subsidised site in Osmaston, and drew the company's attention to the pool of skilled engineers and labourers in the town. They pointed out the ready availability of raw materials such as iron and coal, and the existence of foundries in the town that could convert this to steel for the cars. They also reminded the company that wages in Derby were lower than those in either Manchester or Bradford. The company liked the package and

124   Opening of Rolls-Royce in Derby, 1908.

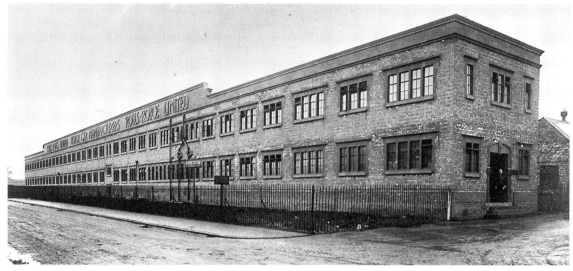

125   Rolls-Royce main works at Derby, new office block, 1913.

agreed to move to Derby, purchasing the land offered to them by the council.

Royce himself drew up the plans for the new factory, but the local firm of Handyside was commissioned to build it. The original factory covered 112 acres and included a new road for access—Nightingale Road. The first car that the Derby works produced was the Silver Ghost. The Manchester end of production was closed in 1910. In the same year Rolls was killed flying an experimental plane, and Claude Johnson took over the company administration, whilst Royce moved to the South of France to work on his designs.

Rolls-Royce gave an enormous boost to the town's employment. Key workers brought into Manchester trained local labour to the firm's exacting standards and in 1914 output was so high that a decision was made to buy more land to extend the works and increase annual production by 50 per cent. Thus the company faced the outbreak of the First World War in an expansionist mood.

The outbreak of war in 1914 was by no means unexpected. Many welcomed it as a release from the tension that had built up between the international powers and also as a way of purifying what was seen as a corrupt and materialistic world. It would be the war to end all wars. War was declared on 3 August 1914, a Bank Holiday Monday. A mood of jubilation and near hysteria swept the nation. On the preceding Saturday the wealthy had withdrawn

their savings from the banks, sending the Bank Rate up from four per cent to 10 per cent, but many were on their holidays. Rolls-Royce put an advertisement in the *Daily Mail* telling their workers to return home immediately and to observe rigid economy. The company realised that luxury cars would not be a priority in wartime, and resolved that, once the last completed car had left the production line, it would cease production for the duration. It advised all men under 35 to enlist.

In August 1914 neither the strategists nor the industrialists had any idea of the important rôle that motorised transport and airborne attack in general and Rolls-Royce in particular would have in the war. Nevertheless Rolls-Royce offered the War Office 100 completed chassis to be converted into transport for the British Expeditionary Force. Eventually an agreement was reached between the company and the War Office that more chassis would be produced and made into armoured cars. Work also started on the Eagle, Hawk and Falcon aero engines. Without these engines and the workforce at Derby which produced them the British war effort would have been considerably weakened, and it was suggested that those who stayed behind to work in Derby should be given special badges acknowledging their effort towards winning the war.[4]

One of the first acts of the government after the declaration of war was to take over the running of the railways. The Superintendent of the Midland

Railway Company, Henry Fowler, worked for the government throughout the war. Henry Fowler was a teetotaller interested in sports, collecting coins and medals, and the Boy Scout movement. He was knighted in 1930 for his service to the railways. At the Midland depot one shop was turned over to making munitions. Staffed entirely by women, it produced 18-pound brass cartridge cases. Howitzer cradles and gun carriages were also produced at the works, and in 1917 locomotives built in Derby were sent to France and Flanders.

As well as providing armaments Rolls-Royce and the Midland Railway Company also provided manpower for the war effort. Those who gave their lives from the Midland Railway Company are recorded on a plaque on platform one of the present station, and in a striking memorial in Midland Road designed by Sir Edwin Lutyens, consisting of a stone catafalque on a pedestal. A further memorial for all those who have fallen in the world wars of the 20th

127 The men who marched away. First World War soldiers in London Road, Derby.

century stands in the market place. Volunteers who fought in the First World War included 260 employees of the Derby Co-operative Society.

Most of the volunteers from Derby joined the Sherwood Foresters Regiment which had a depot in Derby and a long association with the town. The regiment had a ram as its mascot since 1838, each named 'Derby' and numbered consecutively.

The second battalion of the Sherwoods accompanied the British Expeditionary Force, landing in France in September 1914. By October 1914, 33 of its officers and 924 other ranks were casualties. In all, 11,409 men from the Sherwood Foresters lost their lives in the First World War. They are commemorated by the Crich Memorial which stands like a beacon on the summit of a 1,000-foot hill above the A6. Actions in which the Sherwood Foresters were involved included the battles of Asine, Neuve Chapelle, Loos, the Somme, Paschendaele, and Ypres, whilst the 9th battalion took part in the Gallipoli landings. Eight Victoria Crosses were awarded to men from the regiment. One of these was Captain John Green, the medical officer of the Derby Territorial Battalion of the Sherwoods, who was hit whilst searching for wounded in No Man's land on the first day of the Somme. Staunching his wound he freed an officer from the German wire, and dragged him towards their own lines. They were almost back when a German grenade killed Captain Green outright and mortally wounded the other officer. Many other people from Derby and Derbyshire also received awards for gallantry during

126 Memorial to employees of the Midland Railway Company who lost their lives in the First World War, designed by Sir Edwin Lutyens.

the war. Amongst them were Rifleman Thomas Baker of Searle Street in Derby who was awarded the DCM in 1916 for bringing back wounded under fire, and William Frederick Clarke, a member of the borough police force who served as a signaller during the war, and was awarded the DSM for staying at his post whilst his ship the *Carmania* was in flames around him. Also mentioned in dispatches from Sir John French were two nurses serving in France who had trained at the Derbyshire Royal Infirmary.

Those left on the Home Front in Derby also experienced hardship. One immediate effect of the war was a rise in the price of food. The Co-operative

128   The Home Front, Market Place, Derby. There is a recruiting poster on the Guildhall.

Society put up the price of a loaf by a half-penny on the day after war was declared, and the *Derby Daily Telegraph* reported a shortage of sugar and other commodities in the town, probably the result of panic buying as people stockpiled food. The war came close to the town in January and February 1916 when zeppelins flew over, but did not attack; instead they targeted Burton on Trent and West Hallam.

Women in the town worked in munitions works and took over male rôles, becoming conductors on the municipal buses. As the war progressed the local newspapers give some indications of tensions and problems within family life. Long lists of truants printed in the newspapers show that a majority of these were girls from families where the father was an absentee serviceman, suggesting that these girls were staying at home to care for younger siblings whilst their mothers were

either working on the war effort or sick. During the war some companies such as Rolls-Royce and the Co-operative Society gave allowances to the families of their employees serving in the forces, and in 1916 the mayor and mayoress gave the soldiers' wives a special entertainment.[5]

By 1918 there were 16 council schools and 17 voluntary church schools in the borough. The average annual attendance register for 1915 shows a 12 per cent absentee rate amongst the 22,047 pupils attending these schools. Secondary education for boys and girls was provided by the Central School in Hastings Street where girls were taught business studies as well as needlework, dressmaking, cookery and laundry work for 6d. a week. For the same sum boys could learn English, Mathematics, Drawing and Geography. Business studies and languages were also provided by the School of Commerce in Abbey Street.

Most women were eager to help the war effort and even many of the suffragettes who had campaigned aggressively before the war entered into the war effort. But not all—the more radical element of the female suffrage movement continued to campaign and many became connected with the no conscription movement which helped deserters and conscientious objectors to avoid detection. It was this latter movement which led to a series of events in Derby known as the Pear Tree Conspiracy.

The Pear Tree Conspiracy involved four members of a Derby family, the Wheeldons, who in January 1917 were charged with plotting to poison Lloyd George and Arthur Henderson with curare administered either through poisoned darts or in a box of chocolates.

The head of the family was Alice Wheeldon, a secondhand clothes dealer aged 50 from 12 Pear Tree Road, who was known locally as being a socialist, suffragette and a pacifist who was vociferous against the war. She was suspected of harbouring conscientious objectors on the run from the authorities as part of a chain of safe houses which passed them across the country. Charged with her were her eldest daughter Harriet Ann, or Hetty, aged 27 and a teacher in Ilkeston, her younger daughter Winnie Mason, a schoolmistress in Southampton, and Winnie's husband Alfred, a technician in the chemistry laboratories of Southampton University. Alice and Hetty had previously been involved in

129   Victoria Street in the early 20th century.

the successful arson attempt by suffragettes on Breadsall Church.

The prosecution case against Alice Wheeldon and her family depended on the evidence of two government agents who had infiltrated the No Conscription Fellowship. They claimed that they had been sheltered at 12 Pear Tree Road, where they had found out about the conspiracy. It was alleged that Alfred Mason had procured the poison from the laboratory where he worked and had sent it together with phials of strychnine by post to his mother-in-law. The package was intercepted and opened at the Derby General Post Office on the instructions of the government agents. Mason admitted sending the poison but maintained that it was to poison guard dogs at establishments housing conscientious objectors. All the accused agreed that at times they had stated that Lloyd George deserved to die for sending so many innocent men to their deaths.

Alice and Winnie corresponded in a code based on a chess board design and using the phrase 'We will hang Lloyd George on a sour apple tree' as its keywords. When de-coded the letters were found

to contain such phrases as 'Another bugger that ought to be done in is George at Buckingham Palace'. Such sentiments were repeated when Alice was arrested. Indeed at the summing up at her trial she was described as using 'language of the most obscene and disrupting character'. She was known to have expressed her views violently on occasion, having once smashed a heckler over the head with her umbrella at a suffrage meeting in the market place.

The first indictment proceedings were held in Derby. Winnie and Alfred Mason had been arrested and brought to Derby from Southampton. Winnie opened proceedings by making a formal protest about the way they had been treated. They had been thrown into the Derby Lock Up, forced to strip and left in a cold room overnight without their clothes.

The *Derby Daily Telegraph* described the defendants as showing a marked indifference to the proceedings. Mrs. Wheeldon, it reported, was wearing a black skin coat, but her daughters gave every impression of being pleasant looking young women and not the type to commit such heinous crime. The only visible evidence that Alfred Mason was a conscientious objector was his hair which was more than usual length and brushed in a wave.

After the first hearing the quartet were transferred to Birmingham Gaol, and then to London for their trial at the Old Bailey. This was described in the *Derby Mercury* of Friday, 9 March 1917. The Wheeldon family were defended by Mr. Riza, a 'native of India'. Sir Frederick Smith led for the prosecution. In his opening remarks he described the Wheeldons as being 'bitterly hostile to their own country'. He drew attention to the disgusting language used by the two young women who were charged with instructing young children and were obviously unfit for such a task. The newspaper records that Alice Wheeldon answered her cross-examination in a 'silken voice'. She agreed that she had said Lloyd George deserved to die, and that she had written to her daughter suggesting ways in which 'George' could be disposed of. At one point she caused much mirth in the court when 'she explained that her husband had no sympathy with objectors, conscientious or other'. Hetty Wheeldon's voice was barely audible, but the other two defendants gave as good as they got. The paper complained that Mr. Riza spoke in such a rapid way that he was difficult to follow, and it also admitted to some confusion about the exact identity of the government agents.

All the defendants except Hetty were found guilty. Alice was sentenced to 10 years', Alfred to seven and Winnie to five years' imprisonment. At the end of the trial Mrs. Sylvia Pankhurst was given leave to speak to the court to disassociate the Women Suffrage Union from the Wheeldons' actions, and to deny that the union had given the family any money, as was alleged in the press.

Alice was released after nine months at the express request of Lloyd George, and the Masons were freed after two years. They were not pardoned or declared innocent of the crime of which they were accused.

Alice died in February 1919. She was buried in the Nottingham Road Cemetery. Her funeral was reported in the *Derby Daily Express* for 22 February 1919. It described how her young son Willie placed the Red Flag of Socialism on her coffin. Her name was deliberately omitted from her gravestone to prevent sightseers, but the epitaph reads, 'I will have mercy upon her that hath not obtained mercy', a reference to the fact that she was not pardoned. Later her case was taken up by John Clarke, a Labour MP for Glasgow, but as far as history is concerned Alice Wheeldon and her family were guilty as charged. Willie, who was one of the reasons that Alice had joined the no conscription network, ended up in Russia, where he died in the early 1990s.[6]

The armistice in 1918 was marked in Derby in a holiday mood of bonfires, church bells and bunting. The school children were given a holiday, and religious services in celebration of peace were held in the town.

Chapter Twelve

From Peace to Peace— Derby from the Armistice to 1950

◆

One of the first tasks that faced the town when it settled down after the Armistice was to put into practice Lloyd George's promise that homes fit for heroes would be provided for the returning ser-vicemen. In order to fulfil this promise Derby had to build at least 1,000 new houses. The council planned an estate of 430 houses in Victory Road, Normanton. The first four of these were completed and occupied on 9 February 1920. A council memorandum on the history of municipal housing in Derby, written in 1970, shows that some of the original residents still dwelt in these same houses 50 years on. In 1924 the Osmaston Park Road housing development was started but traditional building methods were slow. In order to speed up construction the council started to explore the use of non-traditional building materials and methods. Sheffield council had experimented successfully with houses made of cast iron. Derby's planners were much impressed by their design and the speed with which they could be erected. By 1925 the town had 500 cast-iron houses, whilst the conventional building programme continued at the same time, so that by 1939 there were 7,050 municipal dwellings in the borough. Most had three bedrooms and gardens, and all were built in accordance with new building standards, brought in in 1919, with bathrooms and electric or gas lighting.[1]

In 1921 the population of the borough was 131,151. It had risen to 142,403 in 1931, but like the increase in population earlier in the 20th century this was the result of boundary changes. The 1927 Derby Corporation Act added the rest of Alvaston, Chaddesden and Spondon to the borough and also included Darley Abbey, Littleover, Markeaton, Mickleover, Normanton and Sinfin Moor. In the

same Act the council was given the right to build the distinctive water towers in Quarndon and on Radbourne Lane, Mickleover.

130 Quarndon water tower.

The main employers in the town were British Celanese, Rolls-Royce and the Midland Railway Company. The railways had been returned to the companies from the government in the Railway Act of 1921. Sir Henry Fowler returned to Derby as superintendent, where he remained until 1931.

In 1923 the Midland amalgamated with other railway companies to form the London Midland Scottish Railway Company which was one of the four companies running the railways in inter-war

Britain. It was feared that much of the locomotive and carriage works would be transferred to Crewe, the main London and North Western Railway yard, but Derby remained the most important locomotive and carriage workshops in the LMS, working on new technological developments. In particular Derby works developed the first diesel engines. The first mainline diesel No. 7401 left the works in 1932. It has been preserved by the Middleton (Lancs) Railway Trust but occasionally visits the Midland Railway Centre at Butterley. A companion engine, No. 7106, built at the Derby works in 1941, was seen in 1994 still working at Anezzo in Italy, having travelled there after being shipped to North Africa in 1942.[2] In 1932 William Arthur Stanier moved from the Great Western to become Superintendent at Derby. Stanier was born in 1876 into a railway family. He started work at the age of 16 as an apprentice in the GWR's Swindon works and became principal assistant there in 1923. Stanier is remembered not only for his pioneering work with diesel locomotives but also for the magnificent 'Pacific' class steam engines that he developed.

Rolls-Royce ended the war with an enlarged plant and an enhanced international reputation for the excellence of its work, which led to an increased demand not only for its luxury cars but also for its aero engines. Alcock and Brown's Atlantic crossing was in an aeroplane powered by a Rolls-Royce engine, and Rolls-Royce engine powered planes won the Schneider Trophy Trans-Atlantic Races in 1929 and 1931, the plane on the latter occasion breaking the world air speed record. Royce was knighted in 1930, and died at his home in Sussex in 1933. A year earlier car production had been transferred to Crewe, whilst the Derby works concentrated on aero-engines.

The local firm of Haslam and Newton were also involved in transport, providing electrical equipment for airships. In 1939 Derby got its own airport at Burnaston on the site now occupied by the Toyota car factory. During the Second World War the airfield became an air training school.

During the 1930s the town centre was changing. The outer ring road and New Exeter Bridge were completed to relieve traffic congestion and in 1931 the Derby Corporation Act allowed the council to buy 12 acres of land bounded by the Morledge, River Derwent and Tennant and Full

131 Poster advertising the opening of Derby Airport at Burnaston, now the site of the Toyota factory.

132 The bus station opened in 1933. One of the earliest to have island platforms, its curves help it to fit into the restricted corner site.

Streets. On this area it constructed a new market place and car park and created a pleasant river frontage. The bus station was also built at this time on the space left after the demolition of the 19th-century Shot Tower. The bus station was designed by C.H. Asplin. It was one of the earliest bus stations to use island platforms, and advantage was taken of the shape of the site to create elegantly curved bays out of concrete painted white. A marshalling yard was added beside the bus station to ease congestion inside. The bus station was opened in 1933. In the same year the corporation abandoned trams in favour of trolley buses which had been introduced a year earlier. The first petrol driven double-decker buses had appeared on the town's streets in 1927.

On 21-22 May 1932 over three inches of rain fell in 36 hours. The Markeaton Brook culverts collapsed and flooded the town centre to a depth of eight feet. Shops were inundated and their contents destroyed. St Werburgh's Church was inundated, and the town's archives disappeared under water. Damage was put at £400,000. On 23 May an explosion caused by a gas main fractured by the floods totally destroyed Samuels the Jewellers in the Cornmarket

and injured ten people.

The full order books at the Midland Railway Company, Rolls-Royce and other firms in the town helped to cushion it from the worst excesses of the economic depression in the 1920s and '30s. However, slums and poverty persisted in some areas of the town. The West End was noted for its poverty, but at the same time maintained neighbourhood spirit and a cheerful and resourceful community.

During the General Strike of 1926 the miners in the surrounding areas struck, as did the railway workers and employees of the bus services. Contingency plans were in force to keep the Derby Electricity and Gas Company supplies running. The strike ended on Saturday, 1 May 1926. In Derby the news was met by rejoicing and brass bands. The buses started running immediately but the railways took a little longer to get going and it was not until Jimmy Thompson, a former MP for Derby, intervened that the railway workers returned to work.

In 1936 Derby got its first woman Mayor, Elizabeth Petty. She had been involved in local government since 1913 when she became a Poor Law guardian, which was one of the few avenues into public life open to women at that time. In 1928 four out of 49 of the guardians in Derby were women. The figures issued by the guardians at this time show that, despite the relative economic security in the town, there was a slow but steady rise in poverty during the 1920s. The average number of inmates in the workhouse per day was 509 in 1926, 576 in 1927 and 607 in 1928. In 1928 there were 3,833 people receiving outdoor relief of whom 893 were described as unemployed. In all, four per cent of the borough's population were in receipt of poor relief in 1928, and £58,995 was paid out in outdoor relief. However, it was in the number of vagrants who were received into the workhouse on a casual basis that the real increase in numbers can be seen, from 11,139 in 1926 to 15,640 in 1928 a rise of 16 per cent and surely evidence of the hard economic conditions in the nation that were forcing people to tramp the roads in search of work.

These conditions were the result of a worldwide economic depression related to the end of the First World War. At the end of the war there was a temporary economic boom created by a demand for the repair of the physical damage caused

133   1932 floods.

by the war and a replenishment of diminished stocks. This period of recovery provided employment for those demobilised from the forces but by 1925 the post-war boom had come to an end. High prices caused by tariff controls led to inflation and falling demand for goods, once the shortfall caused by the war was made up created unemployment. Furthermore, the British economy was profoundly influenced by developments in America, which was not only lending Britain money but was also one of its biggest consumers of goods. The inability of American banks to meet demands for foreign currency made it difficult for importers to obtain credit and cut back the demand in America for British goods. The effects of this were felt everywhere.

The Poor Law Guardians also cared for 500-600 children in orphanages and special schools. If they remained in the care of the guardians until the age of 14 the boys were apprenticed at a wage of £8 10s. a year, and the girls placed into domestic service where they could expect a wage of £15 to £18 a year. All were given an outfit of clothes and a bible, prayer and hymn book to take with them.[3]

Life was not all hardship in inter-war Derby. In 1919 a Palais de Danse opened, and the London School of Dance opened branches in the town to teach people the tango and the quickstep. The Grand Theatre, Hippodrome and Empire still presented live shows and there were 14 cinemas in the town including the Regal in East Street, the Popular in Mill Street, the Cosmo in Boundary Road where the first talkie had been heard in 1929, and the Gloria in Chaddesden. The Gaumont boasted a huge Hammond organ which rose majestically from the basement to entertain cinema goers in intervals, and the Picture House had a foyer which was the exact reproduction of the Banqueting Hall of Haddon Hall, the home of the Dukes of Rutland.

During one week in 1939 it was possible to see Loretta Young in *The Men in Her Life*, Bing Crosby in *Rhythm on the River* and Charles Laughton in *The Hunchback of Notre Dame* as well as two different films starring Gene Autry and two horror films with Boris Karloff, *Behind the Power* at the Popular and *Mr Wong at HQ* at Spondon, whilst the Dead End Kids could be seen at the Cosmo.[4]

A high spot of the entertainment year in Derby were the charity concerts organised by a well known and well loved local philanthropist, Arthur Barlow.

In 1934 he presented the world famous violinist Fritz Kreisler in a concert given in aid of the Derbyshire Royal Infirmary and in 1938 Gracie Fields performed in the town at a Barlow concert.

On 31 October 1927 the town passed another milestone in its history when the Diocese of Derby was created and the first Bishop of Derby, Dr. Edward Courtney Pearce, was enthroned in All Saints' Church in Irongate which became Derby Cathedral. Since the 19th century religious groups in the town had been enlarged by the Salvation Army whom the *Derby Mercury* accused of being 'religious rowdies'. There were other new fundamentalist groups in town such as the New Testament Assembly of God and an innovative chapel for the deaf in Friargate where services were taken in sign language. The Methodists had continued to expand their congregations, opening new chapels in Dale Road and Dean Street in the early years of the 20th century, and in Dairy House Road and Blagreaves Lane in the 1930s. The Christian Scientists opened a meeting room in the town in 1928 and a Gospel Hall made of corrugated iron and nicknamed the 'iron tent' was built in Normanton Road.

As the 1930s progressed international tension increased and the threat of war over-shadowed lives. In *The Origins of the Second World War* A.J.P. Taylor sees the post-war period ending in March 1936 when Germany re-occupied the Rhineland, and the pre-war period beginning with the annexation of Austria in March 1938. Despite the efforts of the British Government, war was inevitable from that date onwards, and when it was declared on 3 September 1939 the population had been prepared for the worst. The Committee of Imperial Defence had been planning since 1937 which buildings it would requisition, and as the strategists foretold a war in which the civilian population would face a fierce aerial bombardment, the Anderson Committee had been working on plans to evacuate the most vulnerable citizens from towns and cities to safer areas. One of the first actions in Derby, once war was declared, was to put these plans into operation. Corporation buses were commandeered to take those children registered by their parents as potential evacuees to Chesterfield, North Wingfield, Pilsley, Ripley and Ockbrook. Of course during the 'phoney war' nothing happened and most of these children returned to the town.

The buses the children travelled on had their windows painted out and their distinctive cream roofs were given a grey wash to make them less visible at night. The word Derby was also painted over on the side of the buses to confuse enemy agents. Despite their care in May 1940 the municipal bus company was fined 10s. for infringing black out regulations and displaying a light on one of its trolley buses. The black out made driving at night extremely hazardous, and at Christmas 1939 two trolley buses collided on London Road killing one of the drivers.

As Derby was home to two companies of extreme importance to the war it was considered by central government to be a prime target for enemy raids. Rolls-Royce was camouflaged by having its roof painted. A screen of barrage balloons guarded the town, one of which broke free and impaled itself on one of the pinnacles of All Saints' tower. Anti-aircraft guns were mounted on the race course, and on clear nights a smoke screen was laid down over the town to hide it from enemy bombers.[5]

These precautions were successful and Derby escaped the devastation suffered by towns like Coventry. The civilian death toll during the war was 74, although 4,000 houses were destroyed or damaged. There was a bad raid on 19 August 1940 when three people were killed and almost the whole of Regent and Litchurch Streets were destroyed. Another raid on 15 January 1941 showered the town with 50 bombs. Twenty people were killed and 1,650 houses destroyed. A stand at the Baseball ground was damaged as well as the Midland station, and the bandstand in the Arboretum. In March 1942 Rolls-Royce had a near miss when bombs fell in Nightingale Road. Five houses were destroyed and some Rolls-Royce workers, who had just got off a bus at the factory entrance, were killed.

It is still a mystery why the town escaped so lightly. Theories for this suggest that the Germans thought the town too small and unimportant to concentrate on, so it escaped both the 'terror' raids on industrial centres and the Baedeker raids which targeted historic towns such as Bath, Exeter and York. The position of the town also may have helped to protect it as the river would lead aircraft relying on visible signs away from the centre. It has also been suggested that radar was deliberately jammed to direct enemy planes away from the town and its important industrial plants. Whatever the reason for

the relative security of the town, it was considered safe enough in 1944 to take evacuees from London escaping from the flying bombs.

Men and women at the Rolls-Royce factory were working flat out at producing Merlin engines for the Spitfire fighters, and Hurricane and Lancaster bombers. Over 700 Merlin-powered planes fought at the Battle of Britain, and a Derby-born pilot Alan Feary died during the battle. Work at Rolls-Royce was also proceeding on a revolutionary new type of engine. On 16 January 1936 Frank Whittle, a pilot with the RAF, submitted a specification to the Patent Office for a jet engine. Power Jets Ltd was formed shortly afterwards to develop the engine, and throughout 1941-3 a number of firms including Rolls Royce worked on the new engine. In May 1944 a jet engine named the Welland was put into a Gloster Meteor and a Wellington Bomber. Re-named the Derwent it was in production by March 1945.

Derby had adopted its own RAF squadron in 1917. Squadron 98 became known as 'Derby's Own' and each aircraft in the squadron bore the town's coat of arms. Actions that involved the squadron during the Second World War included support for the D-Day landings. In 1951 the squadron was equipped with jet-engined planes, and the 98 continued its links with the town until disbanded in 1978. The town also adopted HMS *Kenya* and school children followed its progress throughout the war.

The LMS works at Derby were turned over to assembling and repairing Spitfires and Hurricanes and assembling the Horsa gliders which played such an important part in the D-Day landings and the Battle of Arnhem. The LMS works also produced field guns, Bailey bridges and munitions, whilst grenades were made at Qualcast.

Qualcast was developed by Vincent Jobson in 1916. He was a member of the family that owned

134 This sign stood at the entrance to the Qualcast works from 1952 to 1991. An exhibition of Qualcast products can be seen in the Industrial Museum.

the Derwent Foundry which had been started in 1795 by John Jobson of Sheffield. This foundry specialised in the production of stoves and grates. Vincent Jobson worked in the family firm until a disagreement led him to set up on his own. An examination of the market convinced him that the growing number of suburban gardeners needed small but reliable lawn mowers. Quality Castings, as it was originally known, produced manual and motor-driven mowers, and later developed electric and hover mowers. The first factory was in Cotton Lane off Osmaston Road, but in 1929 it moved to Victory Road in Normanton. In 1952 it moved again to Sunnyhill Avenue, where it remained until production of mowers in Derby ceased in 1991. At its zenith in the 1970s the firm employed 760 people and was noted as being a friendly and caring employer, supplying a social club for its employees and sponsoring works football and cricket teams.

The majority of the workforce in the munitions factories were women. They also took over the running of the municipal bus service. At the start of 1940 there were only six women conductors on corporation buses, by June this had increased to forty. Women were also allowed to drive trolley buses, but after a woman driver pulled down the lines in Victoria Street and paralysed the system they were confined to driving single-decker motor buses. Those women who were free of family ties and not involved in civilian war work enlisted. The ATS took over part of Normanton barracks, and the local press show that a recruitment drive for the WRAF held at the town hall was very successful. The local press also has pictures in it of the long queues of people waiting to buy luxuries such as sweets and cigarettes. The war-time ration for sweets in 1944 was 12 oz. per person over four weeks. The weekly food ration allowed each person 4 oz. of ham or bacon, meat to the value of 1s. 2d., and 2 oz. each of tea, cheese and butter. The Ministry of Fuel and Power exhorted townsfolk to '**Stop That Tap Dripping** - Less Water - More Planes'. The poster asked 'Do you know that a hot tap can drip

135   Queues in St James's Street during the Second World War.

away three gallons of water a day wasting the heating power of one and a half lbs of coal?'.[6]

The population of Derby were invited to help with the war effort and spend less on themselves to lend more to their country. They responded by giving generously to the Mayor's War Fund which had raised £6,573 by 4 July 1941, and by offering accommodation to Canadian soldiers stationed locally. An Indian regiment was also stationed at Derby, and an artillery depot moved into Markeaton Hall, where they left on the walls some interesting caricatures of the war leaders. As well as guns on the parks, livestock grazed on the municipal sports grounds, and the Dig for Victory Campaign meant that the town's allotments were enthusiastically cultivated.

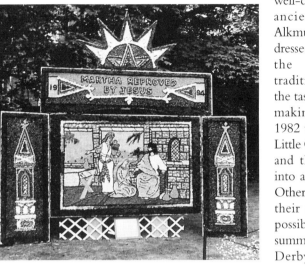

136   Well-dressing at Little Chester.

The Sherwood Foresters had maintained a regimental depot at Derby during the inter-war years and many local men enlisted with this regiment. The regulars of the Second battalion landed in France in September 1939 and with three other battalions of Sherwoods who had joined them took part in the Dunkirk evacuation. Amongst other engagements in which the Sherwoods were involved were the Battle of El-Alamein and the Sicily landings. Of the 26,940 men who served with the Sherwoods in the Second World War, 1,520 were killed. Other Derby men enlisted with the Derbyshire Regiment, which was involved in the Far Eastern conflict. Derby men were at the fall of Singapore and became Japanese prisoners of war.

Peace came at last and on 8 May 1945 a large crowd gathered in the Market Place to celebrate the end of the war in Europe. Street parties were held and St Alkmund's well was dressed in honour of the occasion. Well-dressing is a custom peculiar to Derbyshire. Its origins probably lie in the pre-Christian worship of water spirits which led to homage being paid to their homes in wells and springs by decorating these with spring flowers. Today thematic pictures from the scriptures made of moss and thousands of flower petals are constructed around the wells. There is no record of well-dressing in Derby in ancient times, but St Alkmund's well has been dressed since 1926, with the Palmer family traditionally taking on the task of designing and making the picture. In 1982 the Roman well at Little Chester was dressed and this has developed into an annual tradition. Other areas have followed their example and it is possible to spend many summer weekends in the Derby area looking at these colourful creations. There was further jubilation in the town in 1946 when the Rams captained by Jack Nicholas beat Charlton Athletic 4-1 at Wembley to win the FA cup.

The bomb damage in the town meant that there was a pressing need for houses. Between 1945-6, 293 prefabricated houses were put up whilst a more conventional municipal housing scheme started in Alvaston. One hundred and twelve of these houses were completed and named Thorndike Avenue by the actress Sybil Thorndike in 1946. Work on the 2,660 houses of the Mackworth Estate started in 1950 and was completed in 1959 when the shopping complex on Prince Charles Avenue was opened.[7]

After the end of the war the days of the LMS as a private company were numbered. The nationalisation of the railways on midnight 31 December 1947 meant greater competition for the Derby works, but the Derby-built Royal Scot twin mainline diesels 10000 and 10001 powered the first train to run non-stop between London and Glasgow on 10 July 1948 and showed the superiority of the Derby works. The Derby workshops were also developing diesel multiple units which went into production in 1952. The new Elizabethan age had started, in which the town would become a city.

Chapter Thirteen

Festival of Britain to Jubilee City— Derby 1951-1980

◆

1951 marked the centenary of the Great Exhibition held in Hyde Park in 1851. In order to celebrate this and inject some much needed gaiety and optimism into an otherwise austere post-war Britain, the government sponsored the Festival of Britain. Although the main showcase for the festival was on the south bank of the river Thames in London, other towns and cities entered into the spirit of the times and offered their own festival events.

In Derby the programme of events started on 1 May 1951. The programme included weekly cycle races in Osmaston Park, indoor and outdoor concerts and a festival football match between the Rams and a 'continental team' at the Baseball Ground. St Alkmund's well was dressed and a civic service was held in the cathedral. Throughout the summer sporting and cultural events held the town's attention.

Further celebrations were held in the town in 1954 to mark the anniversaries of the town's charter granted by Queen Mary in 1554. The celebrations again included sporting events, and also guided walks around the town. The whole was dubbed a Cavalcade of Derby.[1]

The 1951 census shows the population of post-war Derby to be 141,264. There was a birth rate of 15.34 per 1,000 in the town and a death rate of 11.74. The population had fallen slightly by the time of the next census to 132,325. Throughout the 1960s the average annual birth rate was 18.2 per 1,000 with a death rate of 14.09.

In 1968 more boundary changes increased the area of the borough from 8,116 acres to 19,282 and the population to 217,230. These boundary changes bought Allestree and Breadsall into the borough and included those areas of Chaddesden, Chellaston,

Mackworth, Spondon and Sinfin that still lay outside the borough boundaries. Thus the 1968 boundary changes set the boundaries of the town that still exist in the 1990s.[2]

The increase in the size of the borough meant a re-organisation of the local government wards. In 1967 there were 16 wards. In 1968 five of these had been amalgamated and the wards of Allestree, Breadsall, Chaddesden, Chellaston, Darley, Littleover, Mickleover and Spondon were added to make 20 wards altogether. Those wards which disappeared were in the town centre, such as Becket and Bridge, which is evidence of the re-distribution of population from the town centre to the suburbs. The transport system responded with extra bus services and in 1971 the Trent bus company's Allestree circular bus route started.

The doubling of the borough's size meant that the council had to think carefully how to provide services in the future, and also how to solve the growing problem of traffic congestion caused by the growth in private car ownership. The 1957 Annual Report of the municipal bus service had noted with alarm that the number of its passengers was falling as more people used their cars.

In 1958 the council published a development plan in which one of the proposed undertakings was an inner ring road that would encircle the town from Osmaston Road to Friargate and siphon off traffic to prevent it clogging the town's streets. The plan stated that the work on the inner ring road could be completed within five years. However, this was a generous estimate and the plan was to take 10 years to come to fruition.[3]

In the path of the inner ring road lay many private dwellings and much of historic Derby. The

137   Old St Alkmund's Church.

138   The new St Alkmund's Church in Kedleston Road.

Siddals area was densely populated and the inhabitants had to be re-housed on the new estate at Mackworth. In Full Street and Bridge Street 18th-century houses were demolished, as was St Alkmund's Church.

St Alkmund's was probably the oldest church in Derby. It stood on a bluff overlooking the Derwent and probably marked the site of the Saxon town of Northworthy. This church housed the bones of its patron saint. However the church had been considerably re-modelled in 1846, and it was thought that all traces of the Saxon church had disappeared. Excavations on the site after the building was demolished showed that the foundations of the Saxon church were still visible. It was a basic two cell church with a nave 44 ft. long and a 16 ft. square chancel. Square additions on the north and south sides of the church indicate to architectural historians that this church could not have been constructed later than the ninth century. The excavations also revealed an abundance of Saxon sculptural fragments including Saxon crosses and the stone sarcophagus that may have held the bones of St Alkmund. These are now in the City Museum.

A new St Alkmund's Church was built in Kedleston Road and opened in 1972. This is a modern building which resembles in shape a ship in full sail. The walls are constructed of coloured glass panels and the spire is made of fibre glass. Some features of the old church were included in the new church. These include part of St Alkmund's shrine and the medieval font, whilst the finely dressed stone in gardens walls in Kedleston Road suggests that at least some of its fabric was re-used in this way.

Unfortunately the town's record in preserving its historic buildings was not good in the 1960s. Darley Abbey House built in 1737 was partly demolished in 1962, whilst the remaining evidence of the abbey at Darley was converted into a public house. Markeaton Hall, given to the town in 1928, was knocked down in 1964. On the positive side the electric power station that had dominated the river frontage from 1922 disappeared in 1971. But perhaps the demolition act most to be regretted took place earlier in the 20th century. This was the destruction in 1948 of the 'Old Mayor's Parlour' which is now thought to have been the largest urban timber-framed building in the country.

Further changes in the town included clearing canalside warehouses and demolishing the canal's pedestrian tow path bridge across the Derwent. The cattle market was moved to the periphery of the town and a car park put in its place. By 1980 there were three multi-storey car parks and eight flat car parks in the town centre.

As work commenced on the inner ring road the council also initiated the development of a new shopping centre. The overcrowded areas of Eagle Street and Castlefields were cleared and a pedes-trianised under-cover retail centre called the Eagle Centre was built. Incorporated into the Eagle Centre was an underground car park with spaces for 800 cars. Copecastle Square in the middle of the Eagle Centre linked a new under-cover market and the Derby Playhouse with the shops. Copecastle Square is a light and airy space under a pyramid shaped roof.

Derby Playhouse became the sole survivor of professional live theatre in the town. It evolved out of the Little Theatre which opened when the Grand closed. Not only had live theatre almost disappeared from the town in the 1970s but by 1977 the cinemas had fallen to three: the ABC in East Street, the Lucky Seven Film Centre in Nottingham Road and the Odeon in London Road which had the Rendezvous School of Dancing attached to it.

By this time however the new Assembly Rooms, built to replace those destroyed by fire, had been opened by the Queen Mother. Here the council promoted a wide range of entertainment to suit all tastes. The Moorways pool and indoor sports arena opened in 1974, whilst the county gaol in Vernon Street became a greyhound stadium.

Industry in the town was concentrated on engineering, but fine porcelain was still being produced at the Crown Derby Works and British Celanese continued to be a major employer. However Rolls-Royce and the railway industry, still dominated the town's employment structure.

Rolls-Royce was producing the RB211 engine in the 1970s. This engine is renowned for its reliability, but despite this, on 4 February 1971, the town was rocked to its foundations when the news

broke that Rolls-Royce had gone into receivership. Panic followed. The *Derby Evening Telegraph* suggested that there would be substantial redundancies. 'Rolls-Royce is Derby' it proclaimed. Repercussions were felt in all areas of life in the town and the directors of the Derbyshire Building Society were forced to issue a statement that the society was still solvent. Despite this reassurance investors queued outside the society's offices to retrieve their savings. Half a million pounds was withdrawn in a single day, and people who were working in the town at that time still remember the vast queues snaking round the Market Place and the feeling of apprehension in the town. Radio Derby, one of the second wave of local radio stations, was allowed to transmit two months before planned in order to monitor the situation.

Rolls-Royce survived, of course. At first the company was taken into government hands, and later de-nationalised. When this happened there was a rush by employees to buy shares creating another run on the Derbyshire Building Society's funds.

In 1956 the last steam train left the Derby works, and from then on it made diesel locomotives and multiple units, and concentrated on developing

139   Workers leaving Rolls-Royce in the 1950s.

the new steel-bodied Mark 1 passenger coaches. The works also developed new signalling systems. In 1965 the British Rail Technical Centre was opened by the Duke of Edinburgh, and Derby has remained at the forefront of railway technology. BREL or British Rail Engineering Limited was formed in 1970 and in 1979 the Advanced Passenger Train was developed at Derby.

The lines previously run by the Great Northern Railway ceased operation in 1964 and the Friargate station was closed. Part of the complex was demolished but the great red-brick warehouses and Handyside's bridges remain and it is still possible to trace the route of the line across the town. Burnaston airfield closed to passenger traffic in 1965 and operations moved to the East Midlands Airport at Castle Donington.

One of the town's two MPs in the 1960s was the peace campaigner Philip Noel Baker, MP for Derby South. He was made a freeman of the town in 1960 and, amongst other honours recognising his work for the town and in international affairs, had a school named after him. The town played its own part in improving international relations in 1973 when it was twinned with Osnabruck in the Rhineland of Germany. After exploring the possibility of being twinned with namesakes elsewhere in the world, and a brief flirtation with the possibility of twinning with Tulsa, USA, the town chose Osnabruck because, like Derby, it stood on a river and also because the two towns had links through British forces stationed in the Rhineland. Twinning with Osnabruck was a chance for both towns to forgive and forget two world wars. The square outside the old covered market is called Osnabruck Square, and there are frequent exchange visits of schoolchildren, associations and civic dignitaries.

The town's ex-servicemen were not ignored at the end of the war. As part of the memorial to those who fell in the Second World War a complex of 16 houses and four bungalows was built in Allenton for disabled ex-servicemen and their families. Known as War Memorial Village, its foundation stone was laid by Princess Elizabeth who praised the people of Derby for their 'wisdom and imagination in deciding to build the village'.[5]

The local regiment, the Sherwood Foresters, was amalgamated with the Worcestershire Regiment in 1970. The 9/12th Royal Lancers which also had links with the town and recruited locally was given the Freedom of Derby in 1972. This was marked by a procession led by a Chieftain tank, and by a service in the cathedral. In 1975 the town adopted HM submarine *Sovereign* which was powered by a Rolls-Royce engine.

At the end of the 1970 Derby had a population of half a million and was larger than many cities. Each mayor at the inauguration ceremony fervently wished that the town would be granted city status during that mayoral year, but it seemed in the 1970s as if the town was slipping down the urban hierarchy. In 1888 it had been given county borough status which gave it autonomy from the county council and responsibility for its own affairs. This status was taken away from it in the local government re-organisation of 1973. On 1 April 1974 Derby became a district council, but although borough status was restored on 19 June 1974 the town eagerly wanted to become a city. It was known that some new cities would be created as part of the Queen's Silver Jubilee celebrations in 1977 and urgent approaches were made to Whitehall that Derby should be included in this. The Queen was to visit the town in July 1977 and the town hoped that she would grant the letters patent conferring city status on this visit, but the council, not liking to assume this, went ahead printing 'town of Derby' on literature promoting the visit. Nevertheless there were rumours filtering out of Whitehall that Derby would be one of the lucky towns to become a jubilee city, and this was confirmed on Jubilee Day.

The council had to take rapid action to alter its promotional literature, and it also produced a certificate proclaiming Derby's promotion to city status for every primary school child to keep as a memento of the occasion. Jubilee day was marked by 300 street parties across the city.

The Queen's visit at which the city received its charter took place on 27 July 1977. The Queen was met at the Council House where the charter was given into the council's keeping and she signed the visitors' book. She then went on two tours of the town, one taking in the Morledge and station areas, the other going northwards from the Market Place to Duffield Road. The day was a great success and was followed by a series of celebratory events sponsored by the council. These included concerts

140   The Queen presents the city charter to the mayor.

at the Assembly Rooms at which top names such as Victoria de los Angeles and Charles Aznavour sang. The first Derby Beer Festival organised by the Campaign for Real Ale was held, and the whole season of events was concluded by a fireworks display in Markeaton Park.

The new city council received a number of charter gifts to add to the city regalia. These included a Royal Derby comport, and three silver salvers given to the city by H. Brown and Sons Ltd., Marks and Spencer and Royden Green the printing firm. The local rotary club gave the city the statue of the Boy and a Gander, whilst NALGO and the Chamber of Commerce both gave paintings to the city. The Chamber of Commerce also gave the city a tapestry known as the Derby Tapestry.

The city's regalia already included two maces. One, the Great Mace, was made of silver gilt and dated 1638. It was believed to have been made from the fusion of two bailiffs' maces. A smaller mace known as the Ladies Mace was donated by T.W. Evans

in 1870, and he also donated the city's sword of state. The mayor's chain, which is in the form of inter-locking SS, was made in 1798 for the Lord Chief Justice and given to the city by Lord Denman in the 19th century. The mayoress's chain was presented to the council by the women of Derby and Derbyshire.[6]

In the 18th century when John Heath (mayor from 1759-60) handed over to William Edwards (the incoming mayor) an inventory was taken of the mayoral goods. These included: 'one great silver guilded Mace, two silver guilded Bowls with covers ...' as well as the town's instruments for checking weights and measures. These included:'one Brass gallow, one Brass quart, one Brass Pint being the standards for Derby Measure, one Brass Quart. one Brass Pint being the standards for Ale Measure, one Pewter Quart one Pewter pint being the standard for Wine Measure ...One case of Troy weights ...two pairs of Scales'.The towns statute books and reference works were also in the mayor's safe-keeping.[7]

Derby's coat of arms incorporates emblems that are symbolic of the city and its history. The shield bears a stag within park palings, a reference to the derivation of the city's name, the town with a deer park. The crest is the Derby Ram which wears a golden necklace to distinguish it from other heraldic rams. The supporters are two horned stags with sprigs of broom on the shoulders. These stags are taken from the Cavendish arms and indicate the town's close relationship with the Dukes of Devonshire and the Cavendish family whose vault is in the cathedral. The sprig of broom was the emblem of the Plantagenet house whose members became Earls of Derby in the 14th century. The motto 'Industria, Virtus et Fortitudo' translates as 'Diligence, Courage, Strength'—qualities which the citizens of the new city had shown in plenty during its past.

141　The City Coat of Arms.

Chapter Fourteen

Derby in the 1990s

◆

The population of the new city of Derby in 1981 was 220,681. Building new homes continued throughout the 1980s, but the 1991 census showed a slight fall in population to 215,866. Much of the development in the 1980s and '90s consisted of private estates, and included Oakwood, the new community of over 4,000 houses situated on Chaddesden Common to the north-east of the city.

In the late 20th century the city council has tried to weaken the hold of the combustion engine through the provision of cycle tracks. Much of the centre of the town was pedestrianised in 1994. This includes Irongate, the Market Place, Cornmarket and St Peter's Street, which has made the town into a pleasant and pollution-free place. In 1995 the council added to the visual interest of the town centre by erecting a waterfall fountain in the Market Place and commissioning a large sandstone ram whose commanding presence stands at the junction of Albion and East Streets, as well as a smaller piece of statuary for the Main Centre showing a boy on a

142   The water feature commissioned by the city council for the market place.

ram. The council has therefore made strenuous efforts to keep the city centre alive.

As well as the revitalisation of the town centre the council has also encouraged out-of-town retail centres. Situated on the outer ring road are the Queensway, Meteor and Wyvern Centres. There are also two multi-plex cinemas which opened in the late 1980s and were the first of their kind in the country. Other entertainment is also offered in these complexes such as American ten-pin bowling and roller skating.

The city council has also put in a bid to the Millennium fund which is looking towards the year 2000 and the celebrations of this date. Building work on Pride Park started in the early 1990s. This is a business park which will be linked to the station and the town centre.

The railway industry went through a bad patch in the early 1990s. BREL was taken over in 1989 by Asea Brown Boveri or ABB as it is known, which merged with Daimler Benz in 1994. They provide rolling stock for a worldwide market. The Derby works also maintain the fleet of 125 locomotives as well as working on new projects. In 1994 Derby became the headquarters of Waterman's Railway which is owned by Pete Waterman, the popular music entrepreneur. The Waterman fleet consists of 260 coaches and other railway stock and a number of historic steam and diesel locomotives including the Flying Scotsman. All are painted in a distinctive dark maroon livery edged in blue and white, and appropriately the enterprise is being run from the Midland Railway Company's Locomotive Manager's office.

In 1994 the re-opening of three railway links in the Midlands gave a further boost to the railway industry. The Robin Hood line goes from

143 The Midland Railway Company's roundhouse and locomotive superintendent's office which is the focus for Pride Park.

144 Midland Railway company coat of arms on Derby Station. This combines the arms of the six most important towns connected by the Midland Railway. Derby as the centre of the network is in the centre of the shield. The other towns represented are Birmingham, Bristol, Leicester, Lincoln and Leeds.

company Toyota, which opened a large new factory on the old airfield at Burnaston in 1992. This has led to some Japanese workers and their families to settle in the city and the city has also become the home of other groups of people from abroad who all play their part in city affairs.

Another milestone in the city's history was the foundation in 1992 of the University of Derby. Prior to this higher education in the city had been provided by the Derbyshire College of Higher Education which had been formed by the amalgamation of Bishop Lonsdale's Teacher Training College, the College of Art and Design and the Technical College. In 1991 the college was granted the right to validate its own degrees and embarked on a modular scheme of courses leading to a first degree. The college had hoped to gain polytechnic status, but the polytechnic tier of higher education was abolished in 1990. Instead the college became the first such institution to go directly from being a college of higher education to a university, and also became the county's first university.

The university operates on four sites. The Bishop Lonsdale College in Mickleover, Green Lane near the city centre, Britannia Mill an old cotton mill in Merchant Street in the Nuns Green area and Kedleston Road. Here the original blocks of the College of Technology have been linked by a fine new atrium which houses refectories, shops and galleries. This was opened in 1995.

The influx of students to the city has meant that the 19th-century residences attached to Bishop Lonsdale College, Lonsdale Hall, the Swiss and Woodlands Lodges have been augmented by purpose-built student housing in Ashbourne and Uttoxeter Roads, and Bridge and Nuns Streets.

In the mid-1990s, therefore, the city looks forward with optimism to the millennium, having grown from a market town to a city. Having acquired a cathedral and a university, it will now consolidate its position as a centre of excellence in the Midlands.

Nottingham to Mansfield, the Ivanhoe line from Loughborough to Burton on Trent, whilst the third line goes from Leicester to Beeston.

Rolls-Royce continue to be a major employer in the city and have been joined by the Japanese car

Appendix

Derby's Villages

---◆---

On one of her journeys across the country at the end of the 17th century, Celia Fiennes observed that 'most of the great towns and citys have little villages as attendants or appendices to them, there being straggling houses for the most part all between the villages and the gates ...'.[1]

Derby is no exception to this, being encompassed within a ring of villages which have gradually become part of the city, connected to it by umbilical cords of ribbon development. However, each village has managed to maintain its own identity.

Allestree appears in Domesday and St Edmund's Church is of Norman origin. The Portway, a prehistoric trackway, crosses the settlement and Roman material has been found in the village. In the medieval period Allestree was an open-field village farmed by strip cultivation. The characteristic 'ridge and furrow' left by this can still be seen in Allestree and Markeaton Parks, and many of the 'snickets' between the houses mark the course of the footpaths between the strips, suddenly turning at right angles to run along the headlands of the field. Allestree Hall is a mansion designed by James Wyatt in 1795.

Closely connected to Allestree in the medieval period was its neighbouring village Markeaton. The

145 Markeaton orangery is all that remains of Markeaton Hall the home of the Mundy family.

124

146   Mackworth Castle—a farmhouse fortified at the end of the 15th century.

entry for Markeaton in Domesday Book shows it to have been a large village in 1086 with its own church and a mill. The church was probably on the site of All Saints' Church in Mackworth. Markeaton was part of the estate of the Mundy family of Markeaton Hall. It was through their generosity that the town was given Markeaton Park which was landscaped by John Eames in the 18th century. At the gates of the park are a cluster of cottages and farms, all that remain of Markeaton village. Markeaton Hall has disappeared, although its orangery and stables remain.

Mackworth which lies next to Markeaton is split into two parts by the road from Derby to Ashbourne. On the south side of the road there is a large housing estate built in the 1950s and on the north the 14th-century All Saints' Church. A little further down the road from the church is Mackworth Castle which marks the site of a fortified manor house and is now a farm. A large gatehouse

with two towers and battlements built in *c.*1495 can still be seen.

Mackworth abuts the parish of Mickleover which with Littleover formed part of the estates of the Abbots of Burton on Trent in Derbyshire. The centre of Mickleover is The Square where the forge and mill once stood, and where All Saints' Church stands facing the Uttoxeter Road. The Square backs onto Orchard Street where Mickleover Old Hall stands. This is a fine timber-framed building with brick infill, which according to tradition was built by a captain in Oliver Cromwell's army. A stone on the house bears the date 1684 and the motto 'Nisi Deus Frustra' which is an abbreviation of a verse from a psalm reading 'Unless the Lord builds the house, they labour in vain who build it'. The same motto can be found under the crest of the Mickleover buildings of Bishop Lonsdale's training college for teachers which is now part of the University of Derby.

Mickleover is surrounded by ridge and furrow, evidence that it was once an important arable crop-producing area. The *Great Northern* public house in Station Road shows where the railway line used to run.

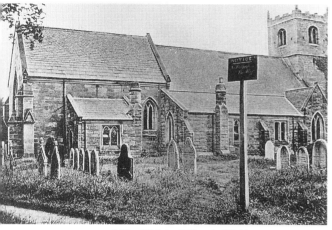

147   All Saints' Church, Mickleover.

Littleover, the other Burton manor, has a Norman church dedicated to St Peter which was re-built in 1335. Street names such as Old Hall Road indicate where the manor house once stood and the Roman road Ryknield Street follows the line of Burton Road through Littleover. Derby High School for Girls which opened in 1892 is situated in Littleover.

As its name suggests, Sinfin, or the 'swine fen', was once a boggy and waterlogged area. In the medieval period it was used as grazing by the burgesses of Derby, and in the 18th century Sinfin Moor was the site of the town's racecourse. Chellaston, one of Sinfin's neighbours, lies close to the river Trent. It is noted for its gypsum quarries which supplied high class alabaster for funerary monuments in the medieval period.

Boulton, where the prehistoric hippopotamus was found, and its neighbour Alvaston both appear in Domesday Book. Alvaston is also mentioned in a Saxon charter dated 1002 and, although its church dedicated to St Michael is substantially 19th-century, it includes a Saxon cross. Allenton, which is Boulton's northern neighbour, does not have such a long history. The first houses in the settlement were built by a Mr. Allen in the late 18th century, and took his name.

Osmaston and Normanton were the first two of Derby's villages to become heavily built-up areas. Development in both came with the railways and both have fine 19th-century churches and chapels. The Derbyshire Royal Infirmary and many of the railway workshops lie in Osmaston, and the Midland Railway Company purchased Osmaston Hall.

Spondon and Chaddesden to the east of the Derwent remained as farming villages until the late 19th century. Spondon was part of the estate owned by the Sitwell family of Renishaw whose members include the well-known poetess Edith Sitwell and the authors Osbert and Sacheverell. The Homestead in Sitwell Street, Spondon is a substantial Georgian house built in 1740.

St Mary's Church, Chaddesden has a chantry which was founded in 1351 by Henry of Chaddesden who was Archdeacon of Leicester. The Nottingham Road cemetery lies in Chaddesden and nearby Chaddesden Lane, which divides Chaddesden and Spondon, was reputedly the haunt of highwaymen in the 18th century.

Breadsall, one of the latest additions to the borough, appears in a Saxon charter of 1002. Domesday Book states that it had a church and a mill in 1086, and the Augustinian canons founded a priory here in the 13th century. At the Dissolution of the Monasteries this became a private house and was re-modelled by Sir John Bentley, a London merchant, in the Jacobean period. Subsequent alterations took place in the 19th century and included an Elizabethan-style wing which was added by Sir Alfred Haslam.

Darley Abbey was also the home of Augustinian canons, who moved out from Derby to found a large and important monastery which owned a great deal of land in the town and also sponsored the nunnery on Kings Mead. The sole remaining abbey buildings in Darley are now incorporated into a public house. In the 18th century the Evans family opened three cotton spinning mills in Darley and built an industrial housing complex for their workers. They also built St Matthew's Church which was completed in 1818, and St Matthew's School which opened in 1826. The Evans family also owned corn, paper and metal rolling mills and had a controlling interest in Crompton and Evans Bank. The grounds of their mansion at Darley have become a pleasant park running down to the Derwent.

Notes

Chapter One
1. Hutton, W., *History and Antiquities of the Borough of Derby* (1791), p.18.
2. Garmonsway, G.N. (trans.& ed.), *The Anglo-Saxon Chronicle* (1953), p.10.

Chapter Two
1. Garmonsway, G.N. (trans.& ed.), *The Anglo-Saxon Chronicle* (1953), p.13.
2. Drayton, M., *Poly-Olbion* (1622), pp.500-1.
3. *Ibid.*, p.474.
4. Garmonsway, *op.cit.*, p.66.
5. Drayton, *op.cit.*, p.270.
6. Morgan, P. (ed.), *Domesday Book: Derbyshire* (1978), 280b.
7. Hutton, W., *History and Antiquities of the Borough of Derby* (1791), pp.23-4; Keys, J.A., *Sketches of Old Derby* (1895).

Chapter Three
1. Derby Local Studies Library, Parcel 183, *Derby Charters.*
2. Darlington, R. (ed.), *The Cartulary of Darley Abbey* (B.M. Mss. Cotton Titus CIX) (1945), pp.21, 37-8, 62, 87, 151-2, 209-11, 215-16, 221-2.
3. *Ibid.*, pp.44, 81-3, 118-19, 123-4, 130-1, 183, 206-9.
4. *Ibid.*, pp.36, 128, 138-66.
5. Manton, J., 'A Hoard of Fourteenth Century Pennies and Foreign Sterlings found at Derby, September 4th 1927', *Derbyshire Archaeological Journal*, 50 (1928), pp.85-9.
6. Page, W. (ed.), *The Victoria County History of the County of Derbyshire*, Vol. 2 (1907), p.44.
7. PRO, Patent Rolls, 2.Ed.II; PRO, Feet of Fine, Derby 29.Hen.III.
8. Page, *op.cit.*, p.45.
9. *Ibid.*, pp.49-150.
10. Defoe, D., *A Tour Through the Whole Land of Great Britain*, edited by P. Rogers (1971), p.459.

Chapter Four
1. PRO, *Calendar of Letters and Papers Foreign and Domestic, Henry VIII* (1535).
2. *Ibid.* (1544).
3. *Ibid.* (1538).
4. R. Simpson, *A Collection of Fragments Illustrative of the History and Antiquities of Derby*, Vol.1 (1826), p.346.
5. DLSL, *Court Book of Derby* (1589-98).

Chapter Five
1. PRO, *Calendar of State Papers, Domestic*, Charles I, Vol. XXXIII, p.131; Hutton (W.), *The History and Antiquities of the Borough of Derby* (1791), p.228.
2. DLSL *Kings Writ to the Sheriff of Derby, the Bailiffs and Burgesses of Derby town* (1635).
3. Derbyshire Record Office, *Derbyshire Committtee Record Book* (1642-3).
4. *Ibid.*
5. British Library, *Pamphlet*, 816 m.57 (1660).
6. Fox, G., *Journal* (1650-1).
7. Edwards, D.G. (ed.), *The Derbyshire Hearth Tax* (1982), pp.86, 89, 91-3.
8. Derbyshire Record Office, Liversage Charity Trust Papers, *Leases.*
9. Morris, C. (ed.), *The Journeys of Celia Fiennes* (1947), pp.169-70, 248, 258.

Chapter Six
1. Glover, C. & Riden, P. (eds.), *William Woolley's History of Derbyshire* (1981), p.24.
2. D. Defoe, *A Tour Through the Whole Island of Great Britain*, edited by P. Rogers (1971), p.459.
3. *Ibid.*, p.459.
4. Hutton, W. *The History and Antiquities of the Borough of Derby* (1791), pp.192-4.
5. *Derby Mercury*, 10 October (1777); *Derby Silk Mill Lock Out Centenary Celebrations* (1935).
6. This book has been produced independently and the author has no connection whatsoever with Royal Crown Derby. Any opinions expressed are those of the author, and not necessarily endorsed by Royal Crown Derby.
7. Derbyshire Record Office, Liversage Charity Trust Papers, *Leases.*
8. Hutton, *op.cit.*, pp.250-8.
9. *Ibid*, p.39.
10. The material for this sections comes from the *Derby Mercury*; the broadsheet collection in the Derby

Local Studies Library; Drewry, S., *Conduct and Proceedings of the Rebels During Their Stay in Derby* (1745); Cox, J.C., *Three Centuries of Derbyshire Annals as Illustrated in Records of the Quarter Sessions,* Vol.1 (1890), pp.194-5; PRO, *Calendars of Letters, Foreign and Domestic State Papers*, Henry VIII (1536).

Chapter Seven
1. *Derby Mercury*, 12 September (1791), 13 September 1792; Derby Canal Company, *Minutes* (1793-1801).
2. Hutton, W., *The History and Antiquities of the Borough of Derby* (1791), pp.297-8.
3. *Derby Mercury* 12 May, 28 May, June 4 (1779).
4. *Derby Mercury* 1779-85; Derby Local Studies Library, *Deeds*, 1106, 1341, 1399, 2144-5.
5. Derby Local Studies Library, Bateman Collection, *Nun's Green Petitions etc.*

Chapter Eight
1. Glover, S., *The History of the County of Derby*, Vol.II. (1829), p.414.
2. *Ibid.*, pp.506-17.
3. *Ibid.*, p.518.
4. *Ibid.*
5. Cobbett, W., *Political Register* (1818); Broadsheets sold at the time of the execution of the Pentrich Rebels; Gurney, W.B., *Trials of Jeremiah Brandreth* (1817).
6. Derby Local Studies Library, Bateman Collection, *Reform Bill Riots* (1832).
7. Derby Corporation, *Police Orders and Regulations* (1836); Hutton, W., *The History of the Antiquities of the Borough of Derby* (1791), p.177.
8. Glover, *op.cit.*

Chapter Nine
1. *Derby Mercury*, 2 December (1835).
2. *Derby Mercury*, 1835-9; Williams, F.S., *The Midland Railway Company Its Rise and Progress* (1876), pp.3, 39.
3. Anecdotes about the early days of the Midland Railway Company at Derby can be found in Radford, J.B., *Derby Works and Midland Locomotives* (1972); the photographs taken by the Scottons are in the National Railway Museum at York; minutes and other papers of the railway companies are in the PRO at Kew.
4. Jewitt, L.C., *On Ancient Customs and Sports of the County of Derbyshire*, n.d.
5. 'The Derby Football Play', *The Penny Magazine* (1839); *Westminster Review* (1835).

Chapter Ten
1. Great Britain, Parliamentary Papers, *Second Report of the Commission of Inquiry into the State of Large Towns*, (1845); *Derby Mercury* (24 Nov. 1847); Cresy, E., *Report to the General Board of Health on the Preliminary Inquiry into the Sewerage, Drainage and Supply of Water and Sanitary Conditions of the Inhabitants of the Borough of Derby* (1849).
2. The Derbyshire Advertiser, *Modern Mayors of Derby* (1909).
3. W. Bemrose & Sons Ltd., *The Red Book of Derby* (1852-1916).
4. Derby Local Studies Library, Derby Poor Law Union, *Minutes, Relief Officers Weekly Reports, Board of Guardians Minutes*; Derby School Board, *Reports and Minutes.*
5. *Modern Mayors, op.cit.*, p.103.
6. Unsworth, W.L., *Seventy Five Years of Co-Operation in Derby, 1850-1928* (1927).
7. *Modern Mayors, op.cit.*, pp.20, 24, 73, 91-2.
8. *Ibid.*, p.73.
9. Keys, J., *Sketches of Old Derby and Neighbourhood* (1895).

Chapter Eleven
1. The Derbyshire Advertiser, *Modern Mayors of Derby* (1909), p.102; *An Act of Extend the Borough of Derby* (1901); W. Bemrose & Sons Ltd., *The Red Book of Derby* (1907).
2. *Modern Mayors, op.cit.*, pp.95, 111, 118.
3. Bemrose, *op.cit.* (1916).
4. This book has been produced independently and the author has no connection with Rolls-Royce. Any opinions expressed are those of the author, and in no way represent those of the firm.
5. Bemrose, *op.cit* (1916).
6. Derby Local Studies Library, *File of Newspaper Cuttings on the Wheeldon Family.*

Chapter Twelve
1. Derby County Borough, *Fifty Years of Municipal Housing in Derby* (1970).
2. Personal communication, Edward Lord, Midland Railway Trust.
3. Derby Board of Guardians, *Derby Union Year Book* (1928-9).
4. Derby Local Studies Library, *Derby Evening Telegraph Cuttings File* (1939-45).
5. Derby Industrial Museum. Examples of Rolls-Royce engines, Qualcast lawn mowers and railway artefacts can be seen in the Derby Industrial Museum.
6. *Derby Evening Telegraph*, cuttings file.
7. *Fifty Years of Municipal Housing.*

Chapter Thirteen
1. Derby County Borough, *Festival of Britain* (1951); *Derby Cavalcade* (1954).
2. Derby Corporation, *Derby Corporation Bill* (1968).
3. Derby County Borough, *Development Plan* (1958).
4. Derby County Borough, *Fifty Years of Municipal Housing* (1970).
5. Derby City Council, *Derby Celebrates the Silver Jubilee* (1978).

Select Bibliography

Primary Sources Mss
Derby Borough Court Book (1589-1600)
Derby Canal Company, Minutes (1793-1800)
Derby Charters, Derby Local Studies Mss. Parcel 183
Derby Local Studies Library Deeds, 1077, 1090, 1106, 1116, 1341, 1404, 1773, 1813 A-F, 1869 D, G-L, 2144-5, 4651, 4662, 4774, 5057, 5132
Derbyshire Committee, Record Book (1642-3)
Liversage Charity Trust Papers, Leases

Primary Sources—Printed
Bateman Collection, Derby Local Studies Library, Material on the Reform Bill Riots (1831-2)
Bateman Collection, Derby Local Studies Library, Nun's Green Petitions
Bemrose, W. & Sons, *The Red Book of Derby* (1852-1916)
Darlington, R., *The Cartulary of Darley Abbey* (1945)
Defoe, D., *A Tour Through the Whole Land of Great Britain* (1971)
Derby Board of Guardians, *Derby Union Yearbook* (1928-9)
Derby City Council, *Municipal Year Book* (1977-)
Derby Corporation, *Police Orders and Regulations* (1836)
Derby County Borough, *Derby Town Planning Scheme* (1924)
Derby County Borough, *Festival of Britain* (1951)
Derby Evening Telegraph, Newscutting File Derby Local Studies Library, *The Wheeldon Family, Derby in the Second World War*
Derby Mercury
Derbyshire Advertiser, *Modern Mayors of Derby* (1909)
Edwards, D.G. (ed.), *The Derbyshire Hearth Tax* (1982)
Fox, G., *Journal* (1650-1)
Garmonsway, G.N. (trans. & ed.), *The Anglo-Saxon Chronicle* (1953)
Glasscock, R., *The Lay Subsidy of 1334* (1975)
Glover, C. & Riden, P. (eds.), *William Woolley's History of Derbyshire* (1981)
Hart & Co., *Almanack and Glimpses of Derby* (1889)
Hutton, W., *A History of the Antiquities of the Borough of Derby* (1791)
Keys, J., *Sketches of Old Derby and Neighbourhood* (1895)
Livingston, A.(ed.), *Muster Roll of Prince Charles Edward, 1745-6*
Morgan, P.(ed.), *Domesday Book: Derbyshire* (1978)
Morris, C. (ed.), *The Journeys of Celia Fiennes* (1947)
Pilkington, J., *A View of the Present State of Derbyshire*, 2 vols (1789)
Public Record Office, *Calendar of Letters and papers, Foreign and Domestic*, Henry VIII (1535,38,44); *Calendar of State Papers, Domestic*, Charles I, Vol. XXXIII

Simpson, J., *A Walk Through Derby* (1832)
Stukeley, W., *Iter Curiosem* (1724)
Ward, J. & Co., *Wards Annual* (1892-3)
W. Winter & Co. *24 views of Derby and neighbourhood* (1894)
Williams, F.S., *The Midland Railway* (1876)

Secondary Sources—Books
Becket, J., *The East Midlands from AD 1000* (1988)
Cameron, K., *The Place-Names of Derbyshire* (1965)
Clark, P. and Hasking, J., *Population Estimates of Small Towns 1550-1851*, 2nd ed. (1993)
Clark, P. and Slack, P., *English Towns in Transition*, 1500-1700 (1976)
Collinson, P., *The Elizabethan Puritan Movement* (1967)
Dornier, A. (ed.), *Mercian Studies* (1977)
Hatcher, J., *Plague, Population and English Economy 1348-1530* (1977)
Marcombe, D., *English Small Town Life: Retford 1520-1642* (1993)
Page, W. (ed.), *The Victoria County History of the County of Derbyshire* (1928)
Pevsner, N. and Williams, I.E., *The Buildings of England: Derbyshire*, 2nd ed. (1978)
Smith, R. *et al.*, *Derby Silk Mill Lock Out* (1935)
Stafford, P., *The East Midlands in the Early Middle Ages* (1985)
Unsworth, W.L., *Seventy-Five Years of Co-operation in Derby, 1850-1923* (1927)

Secondary Sources—Articles
Brassington, M., 'Roman Material from Little Chester, Derby', *Derbyshire Archaeological Journal* (1965)
Brassington, M., 'Little Chester, Derby: the 1926 excavation', *Derbyshire Archaeological Journal* (1993)
Forest, M., 'Recent Work at Strutt's Park, Derby', *Derbyshire Archaeological Journal* (1967)
Hall, R.A., 'The pre-Conquest Burgh of Derby', *Derbyshire Archaeological Journal* (1974), pp.16-23
Manton, J.O., 'A Hoard of 14th century pennies and foreign sterlings found at Derby, 1927', *Derbyshire Archaeological Journal* (1928-9)
Nolan, G.M., 'Cast-iron houses in Derby', *Journal of Regional and Local Studies* (1984)
The Reliquary, 1, 4-5, 7-19, 21-2 (1860-1885)
Riden, P., 'The population of Derbyshire in 1563', *Derbyshire Archaeological Journal*, 98 (1978), pp.61-71.
Scott, J., 'Turn-pike roads in Derbyshire', *Derbyshire Miscellany* (1971-3)
Sturges, R.P., 'The Membership of the Derby Philosophical Society, 1783-1802', *Midland History*, Vol.IV (1978)
Thorpe, A., 'J.H. Thomas and the Rise of Labour in Derby, 1880-1945', *Midland History*, XV (1990)

Index

References to illustrations are given in **bold**